Design Patterns in Modern C++

Reusable Approaches for Object-Oriented Software Design

Dmitri Nesteruk

Design Patterns in Modern C++: Reusable Approaches for Object-Oriented Software Design

Dmitri Nesteruk
St. Petersburg, Russia

ISBN-13 (pbk): 978-1-4842-3602-4   ISBN-13 (electronic): 978-1-4842-3603-1
https://doi.org/10.1007/978-1-4842-3603-1

Library of Congress Control Number: 2018940774

Managing Director, Apress Media LLC: Welmoed Spahr
Acquisitions Editor: Steve Anglin
Development Editor: Matthew Moodie
Coordinating Editor: Mark Powers

Cover designed by eStudioCalamar

Cover image designed by Freepik (www.freepik.com)

Distributed to the book trade worldwide by Springer Science+Business Media New York, 233 Spring Street, 6th Floor, New York, NY 10013. Phone 1-800-SPRINGER, fax (201) 348-4505, e-mail orders-ny@springer-sbm.com, or visit www.springeronline.com. Apress Media, LLC is a California LLC and the sole member (owner) is Springer Science + Business Media Finance Inc (SSBM Finance Inc). SSBM Finance Inc is a **Delaware** corporation.

For information on translations, please e-mail editorial@apress.com; for reprint, paperback, or audio rights, please email bookpermissions@springernature.com.

Apress titles may be purchased in bulk for academic, corporate, or promotional use. eBook versions and licenses are also available for most titles. For more information, reference our Print and eBook Bulk Sales web page at http://www.apress.com/bulk-sales.

Any source code or other supplementary material referenced by the author in this book is available to readers on GitHub via the book's product page, located at www.apress.com/9781484236024. For more detailed information, please visit http://www.apress.com/source-code.

Printed on acid-free paper

Table of Contents

About the Author

Dmitri Nesteruk is a quantitative analyst, developer, course and book author, and an occasional conference speaker. His professional interests lie in software development and integration practices in the areas of computation, quantitative finance, and algorithmic trading. His technological interests include C# and C++ programming as well high-performance computing using technologies such as CUDA and FPGAs. He has been a C# MVP since 2009.

About the Technical Reviewer

Massimo Nardone has more than 24 years of experiences in Security, Web/Mobile development, Cloud, and IT Architecture. His true IT passions are Security and Android.

He has been programming and teaching how to program with Android, Perl, PHP, Java, VB, Python, C/C++, and MySQL for more than 20 years.

He holds a Master of Science degree in Computing Science from the University of Salerno, Italy.

He has worked as a Project Manager, Software Engineer, Research Engineer, Chief Security Architect, Information Security Manager, PCI/SCADA Auditor, and Senior Lead IT Security/Cloud/SCADA Architect for many years.

Technical skills include: Security, Android, Cloud, Java, MySQL, Drupal, Cobol, Perl, Web and Mobile development, MongoDB, D3, Joomla, Couchbase, C/C++, WebGL, Python, Pro Rails, Django CMS, Jekyll, Scratch, etc.

He worked as visiting lecturer and supervisor for exercises at the Networking Laboratory of the Helsinki University of Technology (Aalto University). He holds four international patents (PKI, SIP, SAML, and Proxy areas).

He currently works as Chief Information Security Office for Cargotec Oyj and he is a member of ISACA Finland Chapter Board.

Massimo has reviewed more than 45 IT books for different publishers, and coauthored *Pro JPA 2 in Java EE 8* (Apress, 2018) and *Pro Android Games* (Apress, 2015).

CHAPTER 1

Introduction

The topic of Design Patterns sounds dry, academically constipated and, in all honesty, done to death in almost every programming language imaginable—including programming languages such as JavaScript that aren't even properly OOP! So why another book on it?

I guess the main reason this book exists is that C++ is great again. After a long period of stagnation, it's now evolving, growing, and despite the fact that it has to contend with backwards C compatibility, good things are happening, albeit not at the pace we'd all like. (I'm looking at modules, among other things.)

Now, on to Design Patterns—we shouldn't forget that the *original* Design Patterns book[1] was published with examples in C++ and Smalltalk. Since then, plenty of programming languages have incorporated design patterns directly into the language: for example, C# directly incorporated the Observer pattern with its built-in support for events (and the corresponding event keyword). C++ has *not* done the same, at least not on the syntax level. That said, the introduction of types such as `std::function` sure made things a lot simpler for many programming scenarios.

---

[1]Erich Gamma et al., *Design Patterns: Elements of Reusable Object-Oriented Software* (Boston, MA: Addison Wesley, 1994).

© Dmitri Nesteruk 2018
D. Nesteruk, *Design Patterns in Modern C++*, https://doi.org/10.1007/978-1-4842-3603-1_1

Design Patterns are also a fun investigation of how a problem can be solved in many different ways, with varying degrees of technical sophistication and different sorts of trade-offs. Some patterns are more or less essential and unavoidable, whereas other patterns are more of a scientific curiosity (but nevertheless will be discussed in this book, since I'm a completionist).

Readers should be aware that comprehensive solutions to certain problems (e.g., the Observer pattern) typically result in overengineering, that is, the creation of structures that are far more complicated than is necessary for most typical scenarios. While overengineering is a lot of fun (hey, you get to *really* solve the problem and impress your coworkers), it's often not feasible.

Preliminaries
Who This Book Is For

This book is designed to be a modern-day update to the classic GoF book, targeting specifically the C++ programming language. I mean, how many of you are writing Smalltalk out there? Not many; that would be my guess.

The goal of this book is to investigate how we can apply Modern C++ (the latest versions of C++ currently available) to the implementations of classic design patterns. At the same time, it's also an attempt to flesh out any new patterns and approaches that could be useful to C++ developers.

Finally, in some places, this book is quite simply a technology demo for Modern C++, showcasing how some of its latest features (e.g., coroutines) make difficult problems a lot easier to solve.

On Code Examples

The examples in this book are all suitable for putting into production, but a few simplifications have been made in order to aid readability:

- Quite often, you'll find me using `struct` instead of `class` in order to avoid writing the `public` keyword in too many places.

- I will avoid the `std::` prefix, as it can hurt readability, especially in places where code density is high. If I'm using `string`, you can bet I'm referring to `std::string`.

- I will avoid adding `virtual` destructors, whereas in real life, it might make sense to add them.

- In very few cases I will create and pass parameters by value to avoid the proliferation of `shared_ptr/make_shared`/etc. Smart pointers add another level of complexity, and their integration into the design patterns presented in this book is left as an exercise for the reader.

- I will sometimes omit code elements that would otherwise be necessary for feature-completing a type (e.g., move constructors) as those take up too much space.

- There will be plenty of cases where I will omit `const` whereas, under normal circumstances, it would actually make sense. Const-correctness quite often causes a split and a doubling of the API surface, something that doesn't work well in book format.

You should be aware that most of the examples leverage Modern C++ (C++11, 14, 17 and beyond) and generally use the latest C++ language features that are available to developers. For example, you won't find many function signatures ending in `-> decltype(...)` when C++14 lets us automatically infer the return type. None of the examples target a particular compiler, but if something doesn't work with your chosen compiler,[2] you'll need to find workarounds.

At certain points in time, I will be referencing other programming languages such as C# or Kotlin. It's sometimes interesting to note how designers of other languages have implemented a particular feature. C++ is no stranger to borrowing generally available ideas from other languages: for example, the introduction of `auto` and type inference on variable declarations and return types is present in many other languages.

On Developer Tools

The code samples in this book were written to work with modern C++ compilers, be it Clang, GCC, or MSVC. I make the general assumption that you are using the latest compiler version that is available, and as a consequence, will use the latest-and-greatest language features that are available to me. In some cases, the advanced language examples will need to be downgraded for earlier compilers; in others it might not work out.

As far as developer tools are concerned, this book does not touch on them specifically, so provided you have an up-to-date compiler, you should follow the examples just fine: most of them are self-contained `.cpp` files. Regardless, I'd like to take this opportunity to remind you that quality developer tools such as the CLion or ReSharper C++ greatly improve the development experience. For a tiny amount of money that you invest, you get a wealth of additional functionality that directly translates to improvements in coding speed and the quality of the code produced.

---

[2]Intel, I'm looking at you!

Piracy

Digital piracy is an inescapeable fact of life. A brand new generation is growing up right now that has never purchased a movie or a book—even this book. There's not much that can be done about this. The only thing I can say is that if you pirated this book, you might not be reading the latest version.

The joy of online digital publishing is I get to update the book as new versions of C++ come out and I do more research. So if you paid for this book, you'll get free updates in the future as new versions of the C++ language and the Standard Library are released. If not... oh, well.

Important Concepts

Before we begin, I want to briefly mention some key concepts of the C++ world that are going to be referenced in this book.

Curiously Recurring Template Pattern

Hey, this is a pattern, apparently! I don't know if it qualifies to be listed as a separate *design* pattern, but it's certainly a pattern of sorts in the C++ world. Essentially, the idea is simple: an inheritor passes *itself* as a template argument to its base class:

```
1    struct Foo : SomeBase<Foo>
2    {
3      ...
4    }
```

Now, you might be wondering *why* one would ever do that? Well, one reason is to be able to access a typed this pointer inside a base class implementation.

5

For example, suppose every single inheritor of SomeBase implements a begin()/end() pair required for iteration. How can you iterate the object inside a member of SomeBase? Intuition suggests that you cannot, because SomeBase itself does not provide a begin()/end() interface. But if you use CRTP, you can actually cast this to a derived class type:

```
1   template <typename Derived>
2   struct SomeBase
3   {
4     void foo()
5     {
6       for (auto& item : *static_cast<Derived*>(this))
7       {
8         ...
9       }
10    }
11  }
```

For a concrete example of this approach, check out Chapter 9.

Mixin Inheritance

In C++, a class can be defined to inherit from its own template argument, for example:

```
1   template <typename T> struct Mixin : T
2   {
3     ...
4   }
```

This approach is called *mixin inheritance* and allows hierarchical composition of types. For example, you can allow Foo<Bar<Baz>> x; to declare a variable of a type that implements the traits of all three classes, without having to actually construct a brand new FooBarBaz type.

For a concrete example of this approach, check out Chapter 9.

Properties

A *property* is nothing more than a (typically private) field and a combination of a getter and a setter. In standard C++, a property looks as follows:

```
1  class Person
2  {
3    int age;
4  public:
5    int get_age() const { return age; }
6    void set_age(int value) { age = value; }
7  };
```

Plenty of languages (e.g., C#, Kotlin) internalize the notion of a property by baking it directly into the programming language. While C++ has not done this (and is unlikely to do so anytime in the future), there is a nonstandard declaration specifier called property that you can use in most compilers (MSVC, Clang, Intel):

```
1  class Person
2  {
3    int age_;
4  public:
5    int get_age() const { return age_; }
6    void set_age(int value) { age_ = value; }
7    __declspec(property(get=get_age, put=set_age)) int age;
8  };
```

This can be used as follows:

```
1  Person person;
2  p.age = 20; // calls p.set_age(20)
```

The SOLID Design Principles

SOLID is an acronym which stands for the following design principles (and their abbreviations):

- Single Responsibility Principle (SRP)

- Open-Closed Principle (OCP)

- Liskov Substitution Principle (LSP)

- Interface Segregation Principle (ISP)

- Dependency Inversion Principle (DIP)

These principles were introduced by Robert C. Martin in the early 2000s—in fact, they are just a selection of five principles out of dozens that are expressed in Robert's books and his blog. These five particular topics permeate the discussion of patterns and software design in general, so before we dive into design patterns (I know you're all eager), we're going to do a brief recap of what the SOLID principles are all about.

Single Responsibility Principle

Suppose you decide to keep a journal of your most intimate thoughts. The journal has a title and a number of entries. You could model it as follows:

```
1   struct Journal
2   {
3     string title;
4     vector<string> entries;
5
6     explicit Journal(const string& title) : title{title} {}
7   };
```

Now, you could add functionality for adding an entry to the journal, prefixed by the entry's ordinal number in the journal. This is easy:

```
1   void Journal::add(const string& entry)
2   {
3     static int count = 1;
4     entries.push_back(boost::lexical_cast<string>(count++)
5       + ": " + entry);
6   }
```

And the journal is now usable as:

```
1   Journal j{"Dear Diary"};
2   j.add("I cried today");
3   j.add("I ate a bug");
```

It makes sense to have this function as part of the Journal class because adding a journal entry is something the journal actually needs to do. It is the journal's responsibility to keep entries, so anything related to that is fair game.

Now suppose you decide to make the journal persist by saving it in a file. You add this code to the Journal class:

```
1   void Journal::save(const string& filename)
2   {
3     ofstream ofs(filename);
4     for (auto& s : entries)
5       ofs << s << endl;
6   }
```

This approach is problematic. The journal's responsibility is to *keep* journal entries, not to write them to disk. If you add the disk-writing functionality to Journal and similar classes, any change in the approach to persistence (say, you decide to write to the cloud instead of disk) would require lots of tiny changes in each of the affected classes.

I want to pause here and make a point: an architecture that leads you to having to do lots of tiny changes in lost of classes, whether related (as in a hierarchy) or not, is typically a *code smell*—an indication that something's not quite right. Now, it really depends on the situation: if you're renaming a symbol that's being used in a hundred places, I'd argue that's generally OK because ReSharper, CLion, or whatever IDE you use will actually let you perform a refactoring and have the change propagate everywhere. But when you need to completely rework an interface... well, that can be a very painful process!

I therefore state that persistence is a separate concern, one that is better expressed in a separate class, for example:

```
1   struct PersistenceManager
2   {
3     static void save(const Journal& j, const string& filename)
4     {
5       ofstream ofs(filename);
6       for (auto& s : j.entries)
7         ofs << s << endl;
8     }
9   };
```

This is precisely what is meant by *Single Responsibility*: each class has only one responsibility, and therefore has only one reason to change. Journal would need to change only if there's something more that needs to be done with respect to storage of entries—for example, you might want each entry prefixed by a timestamp, so you would change the add() function to do exactly that. On the other hand, if you wanted to change the persistence mechanic, this would be changed in PersistenceManager.

An extreme example of an antipattern that violates the SRP is called a *God Object*. A God Object is a huge class that tries to handle as many concerns as possible, becoming a monolithic monstrosity that is very difficult to work with.

Luckily for us, God Objects are easy to recognize and thanks to source control systems (just count the number of member functions), the responsible developer can be quickly identified and adequately punished.

Open-Closed Principle

Suppose we have an (entirely hypothetical) range of products in a database. Each product has a color and size and is defined as:

```
1   enum class Color { Red, Green, Blue };
2   enum class Size { Small, Medium, Large };
3
4   struct Product
5   {
6     string name;
7     Color color;
8     Size size;
9   };
```

Now, we want to provide certain filtering capabilities for a given set of products. We make a filter similar to the following:

```
1   struct ProductFilter
2   {
3     typedef vector<Product*> Items;
4   };
```

Now, to support filtering products by color, we define a member function to do exactly that:

```
1   ProductFilter::Items ProductFilter::by_color(Items items,
    Color color)
2   {
3     Items result;
4     for (auto& i : items)
5       if (i->color == color)
6         result.push_back(i);
7     return result;
8   }
```

Our current approach of filtering items by color is all well and good.
Our code goes into production but, unfortunately, some time later the boss
comes in and asks us to implement filtering by size, too. So we jump back
into ProductFilter.cpp, add the following code and recompile:

```
1   ProductFilter::Items ProductFilter::by_color(Items items,
    Color color)
2   {
3     Items result;
4     for (auto& i : items)
5       if (i->color == color)
6         result.push_back(i);
7     return result;
8   }
```

This feels like outright duplication, doesn't it? Why don't we just write
a general method that takes a predicate (some function)? Well, one reason
could be that different forms of filtering can be done in different ways: for
example, some record types might be indexed and need to be searched in
a specific way; some data types are amenable to search on a GPU, while
others are not.

Our code goes into production but, once again, the boss comes back and tells us that now there's a need to search by both color *and* size. So what are we to do but add another function?

```
1   ProductFilter::Items ProductFilter::by_color_and_size(Items
2     items, Size size, Color color)
3   {
4     Items result;
5     for (auto& i : items)
6       if (i->size == size && i->color == color)
7         result.push_back(i);
8     return result;
9   }
```

What we want, from the preceding scenario, is to enfoce the *Open-Closed Principle* that states that a type is open for extension but closed for modification. In other words, we want filtering that is extensible (perhaps in a different compilation unit) without having to modify it (and recompiling something that already works and may have been shipped to clients).

How can we achieve it? Well, first of all, we conceptually separate (SRP!) our filtering process into two parts: a filter (a process which takes all items and only returns some) and a specification (the definition of a predicate to apply to a data element).

We can make a very simple definition of a specification interface:

```
1   template <typename T> struct Specification
2   {
3     virtual bool is_satisfied(T* item) = 0;
4   };
```

In the preceding example, type T is whatever we choose it to be: it can certainly be a Product, but it can also be something else. This makes the entire approach reusable.

Next up, we need a way of filtering based on Specification<T>: this is done by defining, you guessed it, a Filter<T>:

```
1   template <typename T> struct Filter
2   {
3     virtual vector<T*> filter(
4         vector<T*> items,
5         Specification<T>& spec) = 0;
6   };
```

Again, all we are doing is specifying the signature for a function called filter which takes all the items and a specification, and returns all items that conform to the specification. There is an assumption that the items are stored as a vector<T*>, but in reality you could pass filter() either a pair of iterators or some custom-made interface designed specifically for going through a collection. Regrettably, the C++ language has failed to standardize the notion of an enumeration or collection, something that exists in other programming languages (e.g., .NET's IEnumerable).

Based on the preceding, the implementation of an improved filter is really simple:

```
1   struct BetterFilter : Filter<Product>
2   {
3     vector<Product*> filter(
4         vector<Product*> items,
5         Specification<Product>& spec) override
6     {
7       vector<Product*> result;
8       for (auto& p : items)
9         if (spec.is_satisfied(p))
```

```
10            result.push_back(p);
11        return result;
12      }
13    };
```

Again, you can think of a Specification<T> that's being passed in as a strongly typed equivalent of an std::function that is constrained only to a certain number of possible filter specifications.

Now, here's the easy part. To make a color filter, you make a ColorSpecification:

```
1    struct ColorSpecification : Specification<Product>
2    {
3      Color color;
4
5      explicit ColorSpecification(const Color color) :
         color{color} {}
6
7      bool is_satisfied(Product* item) override {
8        return item->color == color;
9      }
10    };
```

Armed with this specification, and given a list of products, we can now filter them as follows:

```
1    Product apple{ "Apple", Color::Green, Size::Small };
2    Product tree{ "Tree", Color::Green, Size::Large };
3    Product house{ "House", Color::Blue, Size::Large };
4
5    vector<Product*> all{ &apple, &tree, &house };
6
7    BetterFilter bf;
```

```
8    ColorSpecification green(Color::Green);
9
10   auto green_things = bf.filter(all, green);
11   for (auto& x : green_things)
12       cout << x->name << " is green" << endl;
```

The preceding gets us "Apple" and "Tree" because they are both green. Now, the only thing we haven't implemented so far is searching for size *and* color (or, indeed, explained how you would search for size *or* color, or mix different criteria). The answer is that you simply make a *composite* specification. For example, for the logical AND, you can make it as follows:

```
1    template <typename T> struct AndSpecification :
     Specification<T>
2    {
3      Specification<T>& first;
4      Specification<T>& second;
5
6      AndSpecification(Specification<T>& first,
       Specification<T>& second)
7        : first{first}, second{second} {}
8
9      bool is_satisfied(T* item) override
10     {
11       return first.is_satisfied(item) &&
         second.is_satisfied(item);
12     }
13   };
```

Now, you are free to create composite conditions on the basis of simpler Specifications. Reusing the green specification we made earlier, finding something green and big is now as simple as:

16

```
1   SizeSpecification large(Size::Large);
2   ColorSpecification green(Color::Green);
3   AndSpecification<Product> green_and_large{ large, green };
4
5   auto big_green_things = bf.filter(all, green_and_big);
6   for (auto& x : big_green_things)
7     cout << x->name << " is large and green" << endl;
8
9   // Tree is large and green
```

This was a lot of code! But keep in mind that, thanks to the power of C++, you can simply introduce an operator && for two Specification<T> objects, thereby making the process of filtering by two (or more!) criteria extremely simple:

```
1   template <typename T> struct Specification
2   {
3     virtual bool is_satisfied(T* item) = 0;
4
5     AndSpecification<T> operator &&(Specification&& other)
6     {
7       return AndSpecification<T>(*this, other);
8     }
9   };
```

If you now avoid making extra variables for size/color specifications, the composite specification can be reduced to a single line:

```
1   auto green_and_big =
2     ColorSpecification(Color::Green)
3     && SizeSpecification(Size::Large);
```

So let's recap what OCP principle is and how the preceding example enforces it. Basically, OCP states that you shouldn't need to go back to code you've already written and tested and change it. And that's exactly what's happening here! We made Specification<T> and Filter<T> and, from then on, all we have to do is implement either of the interfaces (without modifying the interfaces themselves) to implement new filtering mechanics. This is what is meant by "open for extension, closed for modification."

Liskov Substitution Principle

The Liskov Substitution Principle, named after Barbara Liskov, states that if an interface takes an object of type Parent, it should equally take an object of type Child without anything breaking. Let's take a look at a situation where LSP is broken.

Here's a rectangle; it has width and height and a bunch of getters and setters calculating the area:

```
1   class Rectangle
2   {
3   protected:
4     int width, height;
5   public:
6     Rectangle(const int width, const int height)
7       : width{width}, height{height} { }
8
9     int get_width() const { return width; }
10    virtual void set_width(const int width) { this->width =
      width; }
11    int get_height() const { return height; }
12    virtual void set_height(const int height) { this->height =
      height; }
13
14    int area() const { return width * height; }
15  };
```

Now let's suppose we make a special kind of Rectangle called a Square. This object overrides the setters to set both width *and* height:

```
1    class Square : public Rectangle
2    {
3    public:
4      Square(int size): Rectangle(size,size) {}
5      void set_width(const int width) override {
6        this->width = height = width;
7      }
8      void set_height(const int height) override {
9        this->height = width = height;
10     }
11   };
```

This approach is *evil*. You cannot see it yet, because it looks very innocent indeed: the setters simply set both dimensions, what could possibly go wrong? Well, if we take the preceding, we can easily construct a function taking a Rectangle that would blow up when taking a square:

```
1    void process(Rectangle& r)
2    {
3      int w = r.get_width();
4      r.set_height(10);
5
6      cout << "expected area = " << (w * 10)
7        << ", got " << r.area() << endl;
8    }
```

The preceding function takes the formula Area = Width × Height as an invariant. It gets the width, sets the height, and rightly expects the product to be equal to the calculated area. But calling the preceding function with a Square yields a mismatch:

```
1    Square s{5};
2    process(s); // expected area = 50, got 25
```

The takeaway from this example (which I admit is a little contrived) is that process() breaks the LSP by being thoroughly unable to take a derived type Square instead of the base type Rectangle. If you feed it a Rectangle, everything is fine, so it might take some time before the problem shows up in your tests (or in production—hopefully not!).

What's the solution? Well, there are many. Personally, I'd argue that the type Square shouldn't even exist: instead, we can make a Factory (see Chapter 3) that creates both rectangles and squares:

```
1    struct RectangleFactory
2    {
3      static Rectangle create_rectangle(int w, int h);
4      static Rectangle create_square(int size);
5    };
```

You might also want a way of detecting that a Rectangle is, in fact, a square:

```
1    bool Rectangle::is_square() const
2    {
3      return width == height;
4    }
```

The nuclear option, in this case, would be to throw an exception in Square's set_width()/set_height(), stating that these operations are unsupported and you should be using set_size() instead. This, however, violates the *principle of least surpise*, since you would expect a call to set_width() to make a meaningful change... am I right?

Interface Segregation Principle

OK, here is another contrived example that is nonetheless suitable for illustrating the problem. Suppose you decide to define a multifunction printer: a device that can print, scan, and also fax documents. So you define it like so:

```
1    struct MyFavouritePrinter /* : IMachine */
2    {
3      void print(vector<Document*> docs) override;
4      void fax(vector<Document*> docs) override;
5      void scan(vector<Document*> docs) override;
6    };
```

This is fine. Now, suppose you decide to define an interface that needs to be implemented by everyone who also plans to make a multifunction printer. So you could use the Extract Interface function in your favourite IDE and you'd get something like the following:

```
1    struct IMachine
2    {
3      virtual void print(vector<Document*> docs) = 0;
4      virtual void fax(vector<Document*> docs) = 0;
5      virtual void scan(vector<Document*> docs) = 0;
6    };
```

This is a problem. The reason it is a problem is that some implementor of this interface might not need scanning or faxing, just printing. And yet, you are forcing them to implement those extra features: sure, they can all be no-op, but why bother with this?

So what the ISP suggests is that you split up interfaces so that implementors can pick and choose depending on their needs. Since printing and scanning are different operations (for example, a Scanner cannot print), we define separate interfaces for these:

```
1   struct IPrinter
2   {
3     virtual void print(vector<Document*> docs) = 0;
4   };
5
6   struct IScanner
7   {
8     virtual void scan(vector<Document*> docs) = 0;
9   };
```

Then, a printer or a scanner can just implement the required functionality:

```
1   struct Printer : IPrinter
2   {
3     void print(vector<Document*> docs) override;
4   };
5
6   struct Scanner : IScanner
7   {
8     void scan(vector<Document*> docs) override;
9   };
```

Now, if we really want an IMachine interface, we can define it as a combination of the aforementioned interfaces:

```
1   struct IMachine: IPrinter, IScanner /* IFax and so on */
2   {
3   };
```

And when you come to implement this interface in your concrete multifunction device, this is the interface to use. For example, you could use simple delegation to ensure that Machine reuses the functionality provided by a particular IPrinter and IScanner:

```
1    struct Machine : IMachine
2    {
3      IPrinter& printer;
4      IScanner& scanner;
5
6      Machine(IPrinter& printer, IScanner& scanner)
7        : printer{printer},
8          scanner{scanner}
9      {
10      }
11
12      void print(vector<Document*> docs) override {
13        printer.print(docs);
14      }
15
16      void scan(vector<Document*> docs) override
17      {
18          scanner.scan(docs);
19      }
20    };
```

So, just to recap, the idea here is to segregate parts of a complicated interface into separate interfaces so as to avoid forcing implementors to implement functionality that they do not really need. Anytime you write a plug-in for some complicated application and you're given an interface with 20 confusing functions to implement with various no-ops and return nullptr, more likely than not the API authors have violated the ISP.

Dependency Inversion Principle

The original definition of the DIP states the following[3]:

A. High-level modules should not depend on low-level modules. Both should depend on abstractions.

What this statement basically means is that, if you're interested in logging, your reporting component should not depend on a concrete `ConsoleLogger`, but can depend on an `ILogger` interface. In this case, we are considering the reporting component to be high level (closer to the business domain), whereas logging, being a fundamental concern (kind of like file I/O or threading, but not quite) is considered a low-level module.

B. Abstractions should not depend on details. Details should depend on abstractions.

This is, once again, restating that dependencies on interfaces or base classes are better than dependencies on concrete types. Hopefully the truth of this statement is obvious, because such an approach supports better configurability and testability—provided you're using a good framework to handle these dependencies for you.

So now the main question is: how do you actually implement all of the preceding? It surely is a lot more work, because now you need to explicitly state that, for example, `Reporting` depends on an `ILogger`. The way you would express it is perhaps as follows:

```
1   class Reporting
2   {
3     ILogger& logger;
4   public:
5     Reporting(const ILogger& logger) : logger{logger} {}
6     void prepare_report()
7     {
```

---

[3]Martin, Robert C., *Agile Software Development, Principles, Patterns, and Practices* (New York: Prentice Hall, 2003), pp. 127–131.

```
8        logger.log_info("Preparing the report");
9        ...
10     }
11   };
12   }
```

Now the problem is that, to initialize the preceding class, you need to explicitly call `Reporting{ConsoleLogger{}}` or something similar. And what if `Reporting` is dependent upon five different interfaces? What if `ConsoleLogger` has dependencies of its own? You *can* manage this by writing a lot of code, but there is a better way.

The modern, trendy, fashionable way of doing the preceding is to use *Dependency Injection*: this essentially means that you use a library such as Boost.DI[4] to *automatically* satisfy the dependency requirements for a particular component.

Let's consider an example of a car that has an engine but also needs to write to a log. As it stands, we can say that a car *depends on* both of these things. To start with, we may define an engine as:

```
1    struct Engine
2    {
3      float volume = 5;
4      int horse_power = 400;
5
6      friend ostream& operator<< (ostream& os, const Engine& obj)
7      {
8        return os
9          << "volume: " << obj.volume
10         << " horse_power: " << obj.horse_power;
11     } // thanks, ReSharper!
12   };
```

---

[4]At the moment, Boost.DI is not yet part of Boost proper, it is part of the `boost-experimental` GitHub repository.

Now, it's up to us to decide whether or not we want to extract an IEngine interface and feed it to the car. Maybe we do, maybe we don't, and this is typically a design decision. If you envision having a hierarchy of engines, or you foresee needing a NullEngine (see Chapter 19) for testing purposes, then yes, you do need to abstract away the interfaces.

At any rate, we also want logging, and since this can be done in many ways (console, email, SMS, pigeon mail,...), we probably want to have an ILogger interface:

```
1    struct ILogger
2    {
3      virtual ~ILogger() {}
4      virtual void Log(const string& s) = 0;
5    };
```

as well as some sort of concrete implementation:

```
1    struct ConsoleLogger : ILogger
2    {
3      ConsoleLogger() {}
4
5      void Log(const string& s) override
6      {
7        cout << "LOG: " << s.c_str() << endl;
8      }
9    };
```

Now, the car we're about to define depends on both the engine *and* the logging component. We need both, but it's really up to us how to store them: we can use a pointer, reference, a unique_ptr/shared_ptr or something else. We shall define both of the dependent components as constructor parameters:

```
1   struct Car
2   {
3     unique_ptr<Engine> engine;
4     shared_ptr<ILogger> logger;
5
6     Car(unique_ptr<Engine> engine,
7         const shared_ptr<ILogger>& logger)
8       : engine{move(engine)},
9         logger{logger}
10    {
11      logger->Log("making a car");
12    }
13
14    friend ostream& operator<<(ostream& os, const Car& obj)
15    {
16      return os << "car with engine: " << *obj.engine;
17    }
18  };
```

Now, you're probably expecting to see make_unique/make_shared calls as we initialize the Car. But we won't do any of that. Instead, we'll use Boost.DI. First of all, we'll define a binding that binds ILogger to ConsoleLogger; what this means is, basically, "any time someone asks for an ILogger give them a ConsoleLogger":

```
1   auto injector = di::make_injector(
2     di::bind<ILogger>().to<ConsoleLogger>()
3   );
```

And now that we've configured the injector, we can use it to create a car:

```
1   auto car = injector.create<shared_ptr<Car>>();
```

The preceding creates a `shared_ptr<Car>` that points to a *fully initialized* `Car` object, which is exactly what we wanted. The great thing about this approach is that, to change the type of logger being used, we can change it in a single place (the `bind` call) and every place where an `ILogger` appears can now be using some other logging component that we provide. This approach also helps us with unit testing, and allows us to use stubs (or the Null Object pattern) instead of mocks.

Time for Patterns!

With the understanding of the SOLID design principles, we are ready to take a look at the design patterns themselves. Strap yourselves in; it's going to be a long (but hopefully not boring) ride!

PART I

Creational Patterns

Even in the absence of creational patterns, the act of creation of an object in C++ is fraught with peril. Should you create on the stack or on the heap? Should that be a raw pointer, a unique or shared pointer, or something else entirely? Finally, is creating objects manually still kosher, or should we instead defer the creation of all key aspects of our infrastructure to specialized constructs such as Factories (more on them in just a moment!) or Inversion of Control containers?

Whichever option you choose, creation of objects can still be a chore, especially if the construction process is complicated or needs to abide by special rules. So that's where creational patterns come from: they are common approaches related to the creation of objects.

Just in case you are rusty on your basic C++, or smart pointers in general, here's a brief recap of the way objects are created in C++:

- *Stack allocation* creates an object that will be allocated on the stack. The object will be cleaned up automatically at the end of the scope (you can make an artificial scope anywhere with a pair of curly braces). The object will call the destructor at the very end of the scope provided you assign this object to a variable; if you don't, the destructor will be called *immediately*. (This can ruin some implementations of the Memento design pattern, as we'll discover later.)

- *Heap allocation* using a raw pointer puts the object on the heap (a.k.a. the free store). `Foo* foo = new Foo;` creates a new instance of `Foo` and leaves open the question of who is in charge of cleaning up the object. The GSL[1] `owner<T>` tries to introduce some idea of "ownership" of a raw pointer but doesn't involve any cleanup code—you still have to write it yourself.

- A *unique pointer* (`unique_ptr`) can take a heap-allocated pointer and manage it so that it's cleaned up automatically when there is no longer a reference to it. A unique pointer really is unique: you cannot make copies of it, and you cannot pass it into another function without losing control of the original.

- A *shared pointer* (`shared_ptr`) takes a heap-allocated pointer and manages it, but allows the sharing of this pointer around in code. The owned pointer is only cleaned up when there are no components holding on to the pointer.

- A *weak pointer* (`weak_ptr`) is a smart but nonowning pointer, holding a weak reference to an object managed by a `shared_ptr`. You need to convert it to a `shared_ptr` in order to be able to actually access the referenced object. One of its uses is to break circular references of `shared_ptr`s.

---

[1]The Guideline Support Library (`https://github.com/Microsoft/GSL`) is a set of functions and types that are suggested by the C++ Core Guidelines. This library includes many types, among them the `owner<T>` type used to indicate ownership of a pointer.

Returning Objects From Functions

If you are returning anything bigger than a word-sized value, there are several ways of returning something from a function. The first, and most obvious, is:

```
1   Foo make_foo(int n)
2   {
3     return Foo{n};
4   }
```

It may appear to you that, using the preceding, a full copy of Foo is being made, thereby wasting valuable resources. But it isn't always so. Say you define Foo as:

```
1   struct Foo
2   {
3     Foo(int n) {}
4     Foo(const Foo&) { cout << "COPY CONSTRUCTOR!!!\n"; }
5   };
```

You will find that the copy constructor may be called anywhere from zero to two times: the exact number of calls depends on the compiler. Return Value Optimization (RVO) is a compiler feature that specifically prevents those extra copies being made (since they don't really affect how the code behaves). In complex scenarios, however, you really cannot rely on RVO happening, but when it comes to choosing whether or not to optimize return values, I prefer to follow Knuth.[2]

---

[2]Donald Knuth, famous for his *The Art of Computer Programming* series of books, once wrote a paper which included the claim that "premature optimization is the root of all evil." C++ makes premature optimization very tempting, but you should resist the temptation until A) you understand exactly what you're doing; and B) you actually experience a performance effect that requires optimization.

Another approach is, of course, to simply return a smart pointer such as a `unique_ptr`:

```
1   unique_ptr<Foo> make_foo(int n)
2   {
3     return make_unique<Foo>(n);
4   }
```

This is very safe, but also opinionated: you've chosen the smart pointer for the user. What if they don't like smart pointers? What if they would prefer a `shared_ptr` instead?

The third and final option is to use a raw pointer, perhaps in tandem with GSL's `owner<T>`. This way, you are not enforcing the clean-up of the allocated object, but you are sending a very clear message that it is the caller's responsibility:

```
1   owner<Foo*> make_foo(int n)
2   {
3     return new Foo(n);
4   }
```

You can consider this approach as giving the user a *hint*: I'm returning a pointer and it's up to you to take care of the pointer from now on. Of course, now the caller of `make_foo()` needs to handle the pointer: either by correctly calling `delete` or by wrapping it in a `unique_ptr` or `shared_ptr`. Keep in mind that `owner<T>` says nothing about copying.

All of these options are equally valid, and it's difficult to say which option is better.

CHAPTER 2

Builder

The Builder pattern is concerned with the creation of *complicated* objects, that is, objects that cannot be built up in a single-line constructor call. These types of objects may themselves be composed of other objects and might involve less-than-obvious logic, necessitating a separate component specifically dedicated to object construction.

I suppose it's worth noting beforehand that, while I said the Builder is concerned with *complicated* objects, we'll be taking a look at a rather trivial example. This is done purely for the purposes of space optimization, so that the complexity of the domain logic doesn't interfere with the reader's ability to appreciate the actual implementation of the pattern.

Scenario

Let's imagine that we are building a component that renders web pages. To start with, we shall output a simple unordered list with two items containing the words *hello* and *world*. A very simplistic implementation might look as follows:

```cpp
1    string words[] = { "hello", "world" };
2    ostringstream oss;
3    oss << "<ul>";
4    for (auto w : words)
5      oss << "  <li>" << w << "</li>";
6    oss << "</ul>";
7    printf(oss.str().c_str());
```

© Dmitri Nesteruk 2018
D. Nesteruk, *Design Patterns in Modern C++*, https://doi.org/10.1007/978-1-4842-3603-1_2

This does in fact give us what we want, but the approach is not very flexible. How would we change this from a bulleted list to a numbered list? How can we add another item *after* the list has been created? Clearly, in this rigid scheme of ours, this is not possible.

We might, therefore, go the OOP route and define an HtmlElement class to store information about each tag:

```
1   struct HtmlElement
2   {
3     string name;
4     string text;
5     vector<HtmlElement> elements;
6
7     HtmlElement() {}
8     HtmlElement(const string& name, const string& text)
9       : name(name), text(text) { }
10
11    string str(int indent = 0) const
12    {
13      // pretty-print the contents
14    }
15  }
```

Armed with this approach, we can now create our list in a more sensible fashion:

```
1   string words[] = { "hello", "world" };
2   HtmlElement list{"ul", ""};
3   for (auto w : words)
4     list.elements.emplace_back{HtmlElement{"li", w}};
5   printf(list.str().c_str());
```

This works fine and gives us a more controllable, OOP-driven representation of a list of items. But the process of building up each HtmlElement isnotveryconvenient, and we can improve it by implementing the Builder pattern.

Simple Builder

The Builder pattern simply tries to outsource the piecewise construction of an object into a separate class. Our first attempt might yield something like this:

```
1    struct HtmlBuilder
2    {
3      HtmlElement root;
4
5      HtmlBuilder(string root_name) { root.name = root_name; }
6
7      void add_child(string child_name, string child_text)
8      {
9        HtmlElement e{ child_name, child_text };
10        root.elements.emplace_back(e);
11      }
12
13      string str() { return root.str(); }
14    };
```

This is a dedicated component for building up an HTML element. The add_child() method is the method that's intended to be used to add additional children to the current element, each child being a name-text pair. It can be used as follows:

```
1    HtmlBuilder builder{ "ul" };
2    builder.add_child("li", "hello");
```

```
3   builder.add_child("li", "world");
4   cout << builder.str() << endl;
```

You'll notice that, at the moment, the add_child() function is void-returning. There are many things we could use the return value for, but one of the most common uses of the return value is to help us build a fluent interface.

Fluent Builder

Let's change our definition of add_child() to the following:

```
1   HtmlBuilder& add_child(string child_name, string child_text)
2   {
3     HtmlElement e{ child_name, child_text };
4     root.elements.emplace_back(e);
5     return *this;
6   }
```

By returning a reference to the builder itself, the builder calls can now be chained. This is what's called a *fluent interface*:

```
1   HtmlBuilder builder{ "ul" };
2   builder.add_child("li", "hello").add_child("li", "world");
3   cout << builder.str() << endl;
```

The choice of references or pointers is entirely up to you. If you want to chain calls with the -> operator, you can define add_child() like this:

```
1   HtmlBuilder* add_child(string child_name, string child_text)
2   {
3     HtmlElement e{ child_name, child_text };
4     root.elements.emplace_back(e);
5     return this;
6   }
```

and then use it like this:

```
1  HtmlBuilder builder{"ul"};
2  builder->add_child("li", "hello")->add_child("li", "world");
3  cout << builder << endl;
```

Communicating Intent

We have a dedicated Builder implemented for an HTML element, but how will the users of our classes know how to use it? One idea is to simply *force* them to use the builder whenever they are constructing an object. Here's what you need to do:

```
1   struct HtmlElement
2   {
3     string name;
4     string text;
5     vector<HtmlElement> elements;
6     const size_t indent_size = 2;
7
8     static unique_ptr<HtmlBuilder> build(const string&
        root_name)
9     {
10       return make_unique<HtmlBuilder>(root_name);
11    }
12
13  protected: // hide all constructors
14    HtmlElement() {}
15    HtmlElement(const string& name, const string& text)
16      : name{name}, text{text}
17    {
18    }
19  };
```

Our approach is two pronged. First, we have hidden all constructors, so they are no longer available. We have, however, created a Factory Method (this is a design pattern we'll discuss later) for creating a builder right out of the HtmlElement. And it's a static method, too. Here's how one would go about using it:

```
1   auto builder = HtmlElement::build("ul");
2   builder.add_child("li", "hello").add_child("li", "world");
3   cout << builder.str() << endl;
```

But let's not forget that our ultimate goal is to build an HtmlElement, not just a builder for it! So the icing on the cake can be an implementation of operator HtmlElement on the builder to yield the final value:

```
1   struct HtmlBuilder
2   {
3     operator HtmlElement() const { return root; }
4     HtmlElement root;
5     // other operations omitted
6   };
```

One variation on the preceding would be to return std::move(root), but whether or not you want to do this is really up to you.

Anyways, the addition of the operator allows us to write the following:

```
1   HtmlElement e = HtmlElement::build("ul")
2     .add_child("li", "hello")
3     .add_child("li", "world");
4   cout << e.str() << endl;
```

Regrettably, there is no way of explicitly telling other users to use the API in this manner. Hopefully the restriction on constructors coupled with the presence of the static build() function get the user to use the builder, but, in addition to the operator, it might make sense to also add a corresponding build() function to HtmlBuilder itself:

```
1   HtmlElement HtmlBuilder::build() const
2   {
3     return root; // again, std::move possible here
4   }
```

Groovy-Style Builder

This example is a minor digression from dedicated builders, since there is really no builder in sight. It is simply an alternative means of object construction.

Programming languages such as Groovy, Kotlin, and others all try to show off how great they are at building DSLs by supporting syntactic constructs that make the process better. But why should C++ be any different? Thanks to initializer lists, we can effectively build an HTML-compatible DSL using ordinary classes.

First of all, we'll define an HTML tag:

```
1   struct Tag
2   {
3     std::string name;
4     std::string text;
5     std::vector<Tag> children;
6     std::vector<std::pair<std::string, std::string>>
        attributes;
7
8     friend std::ostream& operator<<(std::ostream& os,
        const Tag& tag)
9     {
10      // implementation omitted
11     }
12   };
```

So far, we have a `Tag` that can store its name, text, children (inner tags), and even HTML attributes. We also have some pretty printing code that's too boring to show here.

Now we can give it a couple of `protected` constructors (because we don't want anyone to actually instantiate this directly). Our previous experiments have taught us that we have at least two cases:

- A tag initialized by name and text (e.g., a list item)

- A tag initialized by name and a collection of children

That second case is more interesting; we'll use a parameter of type `std::vector`:

```
1   struct Tag
2   {
3     ...
4   protected:
5     Tag(const std::string& name, const std::string& text)
6       : name{name}, text{text} {}
7
8
9     Tag(const std::string& name, const std::vector<Tag>&
       children)
10       : name{name}, children{children} {}
11  };
```

Now we can inherit from this `Tag` class, but only for valid HTML tags (thereby constraining our DSL). Let's define two tags: one for a paragraph and another for an image:

```
1   struct P : Tag
2   {
3     explicit P(const std::string& text)
4       : Tag{"p", text} {}
5
```

```
6      P(std::initializer_list<Tag> children)
7        : Tag("p", children) {}
8
9    };
10
11   struct IMG : Tag
12   {
13     explicit IMG(const std::string& url)
14       : Tag{"img", ""}
15     {
16       attributes.emplace_back({"src", url});
17     }
18   };
```

The preceding constructors further constrain our API. A paragraph, according to the preceding constructors, can only contain either text or a set of children. An image, on the other hand, can contain no other tag, but *must* have an attribute called img with the provided address.

And now, *the prestige* of this magic trick... thanks to uniform initialization and all the constructors we've spawned, we can write the following:

```
1    std::cout <<
2
3      P {
4        IMG { "http://pokemon.com/pikachu.png" }
5      }
6
7      << std::endl;
```

Isn't this great? We've built a mini-DSL for paragraphs and images, and this model can easily be extended to support other tags. And there's no add_child() call in sight!

Composite Builder

We are going to finish off the discussion of Builder with an example where multiple builders are used to build up a single object. Let's say we decide to record some information about a person:

```
1   class Person
2   {
3     // address
4     std::string street_address, post_code, city;
5
6     // employment
7     std::string company_name, position;
8     int annual_income = 0;
9
10    Person() {}
11  };
```

There are two aspects to Person: their address and employment information. What if we want to have separate builders for each—how can we provide the most convenient API? To do this, we'll construct a composite builder. This construction is not trivial, so pay attention—even though we want separate builders for job and address information, we'll spawn no less than *four* distinct classes.

I chose to completely avoid UML in this book, but this is the one case where a class diagram makes sense, so here is what we are actually going to build:

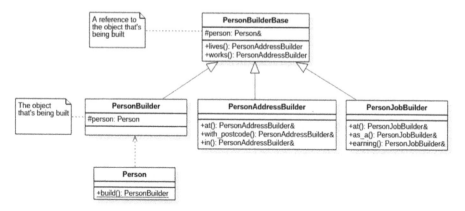

We'll call the first class `PersonBuilderBase`:

```
1    class PersonBuilderBase
2    {
3    protected:
4      Person& person;
5      explicit PersonBuilderBase(Person& person)
6        : person{ person }
7      {
8      }
9    public:
10     operator Person()
11     {
12       return std::move(person);
13     }
14
15     // builder facets
16
17     PersonAddressBuilder lives() const;
18     PersonJobBuilder works() const;
19   };
```

This is *much* more complicated than our simple Builder earlier, so let's discuss each member in turn:

- The reference person is a reference to the object that's being built. This may seem seriously weird, but it's done deliberately for the subbuilders. Note that the physical storage of Person is not present in this class. This is critical! The root class only holds a reference, not the constructed object.

- The reference-assigning constructor is protected so that only the inheritors (PersonAddressBuilder and PersonJobBuilder) can use it.

- operator Person is a trick that we've done before. I'm making the assumption that Person has a properly defined move constructor—ReSharper generates one with ease.

- lives() and works() are functions returning builder facets: those subbuilders that initialize the address and employment information separately.

Now, the only thing that is missing from the preceding base class is the actual object that's being constructed. Where is it? Well, it's actually stored in an inheritor that we'll call, ahem, PersonBuilder. That's the class that we expect people to actually use:

```
1   class PersonBuilder : public PersonBuilderBase
2   {
3     Person p; // object being built
4   public:
5     PersonBuilder() : PersonBuilderBase{p} {}
6   };
```

So this is where the built-up object is actually built. This class isn't meant to be inherited: it's only meant as a utility that lets us initiate the process of setting up a builder.[1]

To find out why exactly we ended up with different public and protected constructors, let's take a look at the implementation of one of the subbuilders:

```
1    class PersonAddressBuilder : public PersonBuilderBase
2    {
3      typedef PersonAddressBuilder self;
4    public:
5      explicit PersonAddressBuilder(Person& person)
6        : PersonBuilderBase{ person } {}
7
8      self& at(std::string street_address)
9      {
10       person.street_address = street_address;
11       return *this;
12     }
13
14     self& with_postcode(std::string post_code) { ... }
15
16     self& in(std::string city) { ... }
17   };
```

As you can see, PersonAddressBuilder provides a fluent interface for building up a person's address. Note that it actually *inherits* from PersonBuilderBase (meaning it has acquired the lives() and works() member functions) and calls the base constructor, passing a reference.

---

[1]This approach to separating the hierarchy into two separate base classes so as to avoid duplication of Person instances was suggested by @CodedByATool on GitHub—thanks for the idea!

It doesn't inherit from PersonBuilder though—if it did, we'd create far too many Person instances, and truth be told, we only really need one.

As you can guess, PersonJobBuilder is implemented in identical fashion. Both of the classes, as well as PersonBuilder are declared as friend classes inside Person so as to be able to access its private members.

And now, the moment you've been waiting for: an example of these builders in action:

```
1    Person p = Person::create()
2      .lives().at("123 London Road")
3             .with_postcode("SW1 1GB")
4             .in("London")
5      .works().at("PragmaSoft")
6             .as_a("Consultant")
7             .earning(10e6);
```

Can you see what's happening here? We use the create() function to get ourselves a builder and use the lives() function to get us a PersonAddressBuilder, but once we're done initializing the address information, we simply call works() and switch to using a PersonJobBuilder instead.

When we're done with the building process, we use the same trick as before to get the object being built-up as a Person. Note that once this is done, the builder is unusable, since we moved the Person with std::move().

Summary

The goal of the Builder pattern is to define a component dedicated entirely to piecewise construction of a complicated object or set of objects. We have observed the following key characteristics of a Builder:

- Builders can have a fluent interface that is usable for complicated construction using a single invocation chain. To support this, builder functions should return this or *this.

- To force the user of the API to use a Builder, we can make the target object's constructors inaccessible and then define a static create() function that returns the builder.

- A builder can be coerced to the object itself by defining the appropriate operator.

- Groovy-style builders are possible in C++ thanks to uniform initializer syntax. This approach is very general, and allows for the creation of diverse DSLs.

- A single builder interface can expose multiple subbuilders. Through clever use of inheritance and fluent interfaces, one can jump from one builder to another with ease.

Just to reiterate something that I've already mentioned, the use of the Builder pattern makes sense when the construction of the object is a *nontrivial* process. Simple objects that are unambiguously constructed from a limited number of sensibly named constructor parameters should probably use a constructor (or dependency injection) without necessitating a Builder as such.

CHAPTER 3

Factories

I had a problem and tried to use Java, now I have a ProblemFactory.

–Old Java joke.

This chapter covers two GoF patterns at the same time: *Factory Method* and *Abstract Factory*. These patterns are closely related, so we'll discuss them together.

Scenario

Let's begin with a motivating example. Support you want to store information about a `Point` in Cartesian space. So you go ahead and implement something like this:

```
1   struct Point
2   {
3     Point(const float x, const float y)
4       : x{x}, y{y} {}
5     float x, y; // strictly Cartesian
6   };
```

So far, so good. But now, you also want to initialize the point using *polar* coordinates instead. You need another constructor with the signature:

```
1    Point(const float r, const float theta)
2    {
3      x = r * cos(theta);
4      y = r * sin(theta);
5    }
```

But unfortunately, you've already got a constructor with two floats, so you cannot have another one.[1] What do you do? One approach is to introduce an enumeration:

```
1    enum class PointType
2    {
3      cartesian,
4      polar
5    };
```

and then add another parameter to the point constructor:

```
1    Point(float a, float b, PointType type =
     PointType::cartesian)
2    {
3      if (type == PointType::cartesian)
4      {
5        x = a;
6        y = b;
7      }
8      else
9      {
10       x = a * cos(b);
```

---

[1]Some programming languages, most notably Objective-C and Swift, do allow overloading of functions that only differe by parameter names. Unfortunately, this idea results in a viral propagation of parameter names in all calls. I still prefer positional parameters, most of the time.

```
11          y = a * sin(b);
12      }
13  }
```

Notice how the names of the first two arguments were changed to a and b: we can no longer afford telling the user what coordinate system those values should come from. This is a clear loss of expressivity when compared with using x, y, rho, and theta to communicate intent.

Overall, our constructor design is usable, but ugly. Let's see if we can improve it.

Factory Method

The trouble with the constructor is that its name always matches the type. This means we cannot communicate any extra information in it, unlike in an ordinary function. Also, given the name is always the same, we cannot have two overloads one taking x,y and another taking r,theta.

So what can we do? Well, how about making the constructor protected and then exposing some static functions for creating new points?

```
1   struct Point
2   {
3   protected:
4     Point(const float x, const float y)
5       : x{x}, y{y} {}
6   public:
7     static Point NewCartesian(float x, float y)
8     {
9       return { x,y };
10    }
11    static Point NewPolar(float r, float theta)
```

51

```
12      {
13          return { r * cos(theta), r * sin(theta) };
14      }
15      // other members here
16    };
```

Each of the above static functions is called a Factory Method. All it does is create a `Point` and return it, the advantages being that both the name of the method as well as the names of the arguments clearly communicate what kind of coordinates are required.

Now, to create a point, you simply write

```
1    auto p = Point::NewPolar(5, M_PI_4);
```

From the preceding, we can clealy surmise that we are creating a new point with polar coordinates $r = 5$ and *theta* = $\pi/4$.

Factory

Just like with Builder, we can take all the `Point`-creating functions out of `Point` into a separate class, a so-called Factory. First of all, we redefine the `Point` class:

```
1    struct Point
2    {
3      float x, y;
4      friend class PointFactory;
5    private:
6      Point(float x, float y) : x(x), y(y){}
7    };
```

Two things are worth noting here:

- The constructor of Point is private because we don't want anyone calling it directly. This isn't a strict requirement, but making it public creates a bit of an ambiguity, as it presents the user two different ways of constructing the object.

- Point declares PointFactory as a friend class. This is done deliberately so that the private constructor of Point isavailable to the factor—without this, the factory wouldn't be able to instantiate the object! The implication here is that both of these types are being created at the same time, rather than the factory being created much later.

Now, we simply define our NewXxx() functions in a separate class called PointFactory:

```
1    struct PointFactory
2    {
3      static Point NewCartesian(float x, float y)
4      {
5        return Point{ x,y };
6      }
7      static Point NewPolar(float r, float theta)
8      {
9        return Point{ r*cos(theta), r*sin(theta) };
10     }
11   };
```

And that's it—we now have a dedicated class specifically designed for creating Point instances, to be used as follows:

```
1    auto my_point = PointFactory::NewCartesian(3, 4);
```

Inner Factory

An inner factory is simply a factory that is an inner class within the type it creates. To be fair, inner factories are typical artifacts of C#, Java, and other languages that lack the friend keyword, but there's no reason one cannot have it in C++, too.

The reason why inner factories exist is because inner classes can access the outer class' private members and, conversely, an outer class can access an inner class' private members. This means that our Point class can also be defined as follows:

```
1    struct Point
2    {
3    private:
4      Point(float x, float y) : x(x), y(y) {}
5
6      struct PointFactory
7      {
8      private:
9        PointFactory() {}
10     public:
11       static Point NewCartesian(float x, float y)
12       {
13         return { x,y };
14       }
15       static Point NewPolar(float r, float theta)
16       {
17         return{ r*cos(theta), r*sin(theta) };
18       }
19     };
20   public:
21     float x, y;
```

```
22     static PointFactory Factory;
23   };
```

Okay, so what's going on here? Well, we've stuck the factory right into the class the factory creates. This is convenient if a factory only works with one single type, and not so convenient if a factory relies on several types (and pretty much impossible if it needs their `private` members, too).

You'll notice that I'm being sly here: the entire factory is inside a `private` block and, furthermore, its constructor is marked as `private` too. Essentially, even though we *could* expose this factory as `Point::PointFactory`, that's quite a mouthful. Instead, I define a static member called `Factory`. This allows us to use the factory as

```
1    auto pp = Point::Factory.NewCartesian(2, 3);
```

If, for some reason, you don't like mixing `::` and `.`, you can, of course, change the code such that you use `::` everywhere. The two says to do this are:

- Make the factory public, which lets you write

```
1    Point::PointFactory::NewXxx(...)`
```

- If you don't like the word `Point` appearing twice in the preceding, you can `typedef PointFactory Factory` and then simply write `Point::Factory::NewXxx(...)`. This is probably the most sensible syntax one can come up with. Or just call the inner factory `Factory`, which kind of solves the problem once and for all... unless you decide to factor it out later on.

The decision of whether or not to have an inner factory depends largely on how you like to organize your code. However, exposing the factory from the original object drastically improves the usability of the API. If I find a type called `Point` with a `private` constructor, how would I be able to tell that the class is meant to be used? Well, I wouldn't unless `Person::` gives me something meaningful in the code completion listing.

Abstract Factory

So far, we've been looking at the construction of a single object. Sometimes, you might be involved in the creation of families of objects. This is actually a pretty *rare* case, so unlike Factory Method and just plain old Factory pattern, Abstract Factory is a pattern that only pops its head in complicated systems. We need to talk about it, regardless, primarily for historical reasons.

Here's a simple scenario: suppose you are working at a café that serves tea and coffee. These two hot beverages are made through entirely different apparatus that we can both model as factories, of sorts. Tea and coffee can actually be served both hot or hold, but let's focus on the hot variety. First of all, we can define what a HotDrink is:

```
1    struct HotDrink
2    {
3      virtual void prepare(int volume) = 0;
4    };
```

The function prepare is what we would call to prepare a hot drink with a specific volume. For example, for a type Tea, it would be implemented as

```
1    struct Tea : HotDrink
2    {
3
4      void prepare(int volume) override
5      {
6        cout << "Take tea bag, boil water, pour " << volume <<
7        "ml, add some lemon" << endl;
8      }
9    };
```

And similarly for the Coffee type. At this point, we could write a hypothetical make_drink() function that would take the *name* of a drink and make that drink. Given a discrete set of cases, it can look rather tedious:

```
1    unique_ptr<HotDrink> make_drink(string type)
2    {
3      unique_ptr<HotDrink> drink;
4      if (type == "tea")
5      {
6        drink = make_unique<Tea>();
7        drink->prepare(200);
8      }
9      else
10     {
11       drink = make_unique<Coffee>();
12       drink->prepare(50);
13     }
14     return drink;
15   }
```

Now, remember, different drinks are made by different machinery. In our case, we're interested in hot drinks, which we'll model through the aptly named Hot-DrinkFactory:

```
1    struct HotDrinkFactory
2    {
3      virtual unique_ptr<HotDrink> make() const = 0;
4    };
```

This type happens to be an *Abstract Factory*: it's a factory with a specific interface, but it's abstract, which means that even though it can feature as a function argument, for example, we would need concrete implementations to actually make the drinks. For example, in the case of making Coffee, we could write

```
1    struct CoffeeFactory : HotDrinkFactory
2    {
3      unique_ptr<HotDrink> make() const override
4      {
5        return make_unique<Coffee>();
6      }
7    }
```

And the same goes for TeaFactory, as before. Now, suppose we want to define a higher level interface for making different drinks, hot or cold. We could make a type called DrinkFactory that would itself contain references to the various factories that are available:

```
1    class DrinkFactory
2    {
3      map<string, unique_ptr<HotDrinkFactory>> hot_factories;
4    public:
5      DrinkFactory()
6      {
7        hot_factories["coffee"] = make_unique<CoffeeFactory>();
8        hot_factories["tea"] = make_unique<TeaFactory>();
9      }
10
11     unique_ptr<HotDrink> make_drink(const string& name)
12     {
13       auto drink = hot_factories[name]->make();
14       drink->prepare(200); // oops!
15       return drink;
16     }
17   };
```

Here I've made an assumption that we want drinks dispensed based on their name rather than some integer or enum member. We simply make a map of strings and the associated factories: the actual factory type is HotDrinkFactory (our Abstract Factory), and we store them through smart pointers rather than directly (makes sense, because we want to prevent object slicing).

Now, when someone wants a drink, we find the relevant factory (think of a coffee shop assistant walking to the right machine), create the beverage, prepare exactly the volume required (I've set it to a constant in the preceding; feel free to promote it to a parameter) and then return the relevant drink. That's all there is to it.

Functional Factory

One last thing I wanted to mention: when we typically use the term *factory* we typically mean one of two things:

- A class that knows how to create objects
- A function that, when called, creates an object

The second option is not just a Factory Method in a classical sense. If someone passes in a std::function that returns a type T into some function, this is typically referred to as a Factory, not a Factory Method. This may seem a little weird, but when you consider the idea that a Method is synonymous with Member Function, it makes a bit more sense.

Luckily for us, functions can be stored in variables, which means that instead of just storing a pointer to the factory (as we did inDrinkFactory earlier), we can internalize the process of preparing exactly 200 ml of a liquid. This is done by switching from factories to simply using function blocks, for example:

```
1   class DrinkWithVolumeFactory
2   {
3     map<string, function<unique_ptr<HotDrink>()>> factories;
```

```
4    public:
5      DrinkWithVolumeFactory()
6      {
7        factories["tea"] = [] {
8          auto tea = make_unique<Tea>();
9          tea->prepare(200);
10         return tea;
11       }; // similar for Coffee
12     }
13   };
```

Of course, having taken this approach, we are now reduced to calling the stored factory directly, that is:

```
1    inline unique_ptr<HotDrink>
2    DrinkWithVolumeFactory::make_drink(const string& name)
3    {
4      return factories[name]();
5    }
```

And this can then be used as before.

Summary

Let's recap the terminology:

- A *factory method* is a class member that acts as a way of creating object. It typically replaces a constructor.

- A *factory* is typically a separate class that knows how to construct objects, though if you pass a function (as in std::function or similar) that constructs objects, this argument is also called a factory.

- An *abstract factory* is, as its name suggests, an abstract class that can be inherited by concrete classes that offer a family of types. Abstract factories are rare in the wild.

A factory has several critical advantages over a constructor call, namely:

- A factory can say *no*, meaning that instead of actually returning an object it can return, for example, a `nullptr`.

- Naming is better and unconstrained, unlike constructor name.

- A single factory can make objects of many different types.

- A factory can exhibit polymorphic behavior, instantiating a class and returning it through its base class' reference or pointer.

- A factory can implement caching and other storage optimizations; it is also a natural choice for approaches such as pooling or the Singleton pattern (more on this in Chapter 5).

Factory is different from Builder in that, with a Factory, you typically create an object in one go, whereas with Builder, you construct the object piecewise by providing information in parts.

CHAPTER 4

Prototype

Think about something you use every day, like a car or a mobile phone. Chances are, it wasn't designed from scratch; instead, the manufacturer chose an *existing* design, made some improvements, made it visually distinctive from the old design (so people could show off), and started selling it, retiring the old product. It's a natural state of affairs, and in the software world, we get a similar situation: sometimes, instead of creating an entire object from scratch (the Factory and Builder patterns can help here), you want to take a preconstructed object and either use a copy of it (which is easy) or, alternatively, customize it a little.

And this leads us to the idea of having a Prototype: a model object that we can make copies of, customize those copies, and then use them. The challenge of the Prototype pattern is really the copying part; everything else is easy.

Object Constrution

Most of object construction happens using, ahem, constructors. But if you've got an object configured already, why not simply *copy* that object instead of creating an identical one? This is particularly relevant if you've had to apply the Builder pattern to simplify piecewise object construction.

© Dmitri Nesteruk 2018
D. Nesteruk, *Design Patterns in Modern C++*, https://doi.org/10.1007/978-1-4842-3603-1_4

Let's consider a simple example, but one that clearly shows duplication:

```
1   Contact john{ "John Doe", Address{"123 East Dr",
    "London", 10 } };
2   Contact jane{ "Jane Doe", Address{"123 East Dr",
    "London", 11 } };
```

You can see what's happening here. Both john and jane work in the same building, but in different offices. Many other people might work at 123 East Dr in London, so what if we want to avoid repeated initialization of the address. How can we do it?

The fact is, the Prototype pattern is all about object copying. And, of course, we do *not* have a uniform way of actually copying an object, but there are options, and we'll choose some of them.

Ordinary Duplication

If what you are copying is a value, and the object you're copying stores everything through values, there's no problem. For example, if you define Contact and Address from the preceding example as

```
1   struct Address
2   {
3       string street, city;
4       int suite;
5   }
6   struct Contact
7   {
8       string name;
9       Address address;
10  }
```

there's absolutely no issue in writing something like

```
1    // here is the prototype:
2    Contact worker{"", Address{"123 East Dr", "London", 0}};
3
4    // make a copy of prototype and customize it
5    Contact john = worker;
6    john.name = "John Doe";
7    john.address.suite = 10;
```

In practice, this is quite a rare occurence. In many cases, the inner Address object would be, for example, a pointer:

```
1    struct Contact
2    {
3      string name;
4      Address *address; // pointer (or e.g., shared_ptr)
5    }
```

This throws a wrench in the works because now the line Contact john = prototype copies the pointer, and now both john and prototype and every other copy of the prototype share the same address. Which we *definitely* do not want.

Duplication via Copy Construction

The simplest way of avoiding duplication is to ensure that copy constructors are defined on all the constituent parts (in this case, Contact and Address) that make up the object. For example, if we go with the idea of storing the address via an owned pointer, that is:

```
1    struct Contact
2    {
3      string name;
```

```
4      Address* address;
5    }
```

then we would need to create a copy constructor. There are actually two
ways to do this, in our case. The head-on approach would look something
like this:

```
1    Contact(const Contact& other)
2      : name{other.name}
3      //, address{ new Address{*other.address} }
4    {
5      address = new Address(
6        other.address->street,
7        other.address->city,
8        other.address->suite
9      );
10   }
```

Unfortunately, the preceding approach is not sufficiently generic.
It will certainly work in this case (provided Address has a constructor that
initializes all its members), but what if Address decides to fragment its
street part into an object consisting of street name, house number, and
additional information? Then we'll have that same copying problem again.

A sensible thing to do here would be to also define a copy constructor
on Address. In our case, it's rather trivial:

```
1    Address(const string& street, const string& city, const int
     suite)
2      : street{street},
3        city{city},
4        suite{suite} {}
```

Now we can rewrite the Contact constructor to reuse this copy constructor:

```
1   Contact(const Contact& other)
2     : name{other.name}
3     , address{ new Address{*other.address} }
4     {}
```

Mind you, if you use ReSharper's generator for **Copy and Move Operations**, it will also give you operator= which, in our case, would be defined as

```
1   Contact& operator=(const Contact& other)
2   {
3     if (this == &other)
4       return *this;
5     name = other.name;
6     address = other.address;
7     return *this;
8   }
```

That's much better. Now, we can construct a prototype as before and then reuse it:

```
1   Contact worker{"", new Address{"123 East Dr", "London", 0}};
2   Contact john{worker}; // or: Contact john = worker;
3   john.name = "John";
4   john.suite = 10;
```

This approach works, and it works well. The only real issue here, and one that cannot be solved easily, is the amount of extra effort required to implement all those copy constructors. Granted, a tool like ReSharper makes quick work of most scenarios, but there are plenty of caveats. For example, what do you think would happen if I wrote

```
1   Contact john = worker;
```

and forgot to implement copy assignment for `Address` (but not for
`Contact`)? That's right, the program would still compile. It's a little better
with copy constructors because if you try to call one and it's missing,
you get an error, whereas `operator =` is ubiquitous even if you haven't
specified correct operation.

Here is another issue: suppose you start using something like a double
pointer (e.g., `void**`)? Or a `unique_ptr`? Even with all their magic, tools
like ReSharper and CLion are unlikely to generate correct code at this
point, so rapid firing code generation on these types might not always be
the best idea.

You can reduce the entropy somewhat by sticking to copy constructors
and not generating copy assignment operators. Another option would be
to ditch copy constructors also in favor of something like

```
1    template <typename T> struct Cloneable
2    {
3      virtual T clone() const = 0;
4    }
```

and then proceed to implement this interface and call `prototype.clone()`
whenever you need an actual copy. This actually communicates intent a
little bit better than copy constructors/assignment.

Regardless of which option you go for, the takeaway here is that the
approach works, but *will* become a bit tedious if your object graph is very
complicated.

Serialization

Designers of other programming languages have encountered this same
problem of having to explicitly define copying operations on entire
object graphs, and quickly realized that a class needs to be "trivially

serializable"—that, by default, you should be able to take a class and write it to a file, for example, without having to anoint the class with any traits (well, maybe an attribute or two, at most).

Why is this relevant to the problem at hand? Because if you can serialize something to a file or to memory, you can then deserialize it, preserving all the information, including all the dependent objects. Isn't this convenient? Well...

Unlike other programming languages, unfortunately, C++ does not offer us any free lunch when it comes to serialization. We cannot, for example, take a complicated object graph and serialize the entire graph to a file. Why not? Well, in other programming languages, compiled binaries include not just executable code but plenty of metadata, and serialization is possible through a feature called *reflection*—so far unavailable in C++.

If we want serialization then, just like with explicit copying operations, we need to implement it ourselves. Luckily, rather than fiddling bits and thinking up ways of serializing an std::string, we can use a ready-made library called Boost.Serialization to take care of some of this for us. Here's an example of how we would add serialization support to an Address type:

```
1   struct Address
2   {
3     string street;
4     string city;
5     int suite;
6   private:
7     friend class boost::serialization::access;
8     template<class Ar> void serialize(Ar& ar, const unsigned int version)
9     {
10      ar & street;
11      ar & city;
12      ar & suite;
13    }
14  }
```

This may seem a bit backward, to be honest, but the net result is that we've specified, using the & operator, all the parts of the Address that we would need to write to wherever we would be saving the object. Note that the preceding code is a member function for both saving and loading the data. It *is* possible to tell Boost to perform different operations on saving and loading, but this isn't particularly relevant to our prototyping needs.

Now, we also need to perform the same manipulation for the Contact type. Here we go:

```
1    struct Contact
2    {
3      string name;
4      Address* address = nullptr;
5    private:
6      friend class boost::serialization::access;
7      template<class Ar> void serialize(Ar& ar, const unsigned
       int version)
8      {
9        ar & name;
10       ar & address; // no *
11     }
12   };
```

The structure of the preceding serialize() function is more or less the same, but notice one interesting thing: instead of accessing the address as ar & *address, we still serialize it as ar & address, without dereferencing the pointer. Boost is smart enough to figure out what's going on, and will serialize/deserialize things just fine even if address is set to nullptr.

So, if you want to implement the Prototype pattern this way, you need to implement serialize() on every single possible type that may appear in the object graph. But if you do, what you can now do is define a way of cloning an object via serialization/deserialization:

```
1    auto clone = [](const Contact& c)
2    {
3      // 1. Serialize the contact
4      ostringstream oss;
5      boost::archive::text_oarchive oa(oss);
6      oa << c;
7      string s = oss.str();
8
9      // 2. Deserialize the contact
10     istringstream iss(oss.str());
11     boost::archive::text_iarchive ia(iss);
12     Contact result;
13     ia >> result;
14     return result;
15   };
```

And now, having a contact called john, you can simply write

```
1    Contact jane = clone(john);
2    jane.name = "Jane"; // and so on
```

and then customize jane to your heart's content.

Prototype Factory

If you have predefined objects that you want to replicate, where do you actually store them? A global variable? Perhaps. In fact, suppose our company has both main and auxiliary offices. We can declare global variables like this:

```
1   Contact main{ "", new Address{ "123 East Dr", "London", 0 } };
2   Contact aux{ "", new Address{ "123B East Dr", "London", 0 } };
```

We could, for example, stick these definitions into Contact.h so anyone using the Contact class would be able to take one of these global variables and make a copy of them. But a more sensible approach would be to have some sort of dedicated class that would store the prototypes and hand out customized copies of said prototypes on demand. This would allow us additional flexibility: for example, we could make utility functions and hand out properly initialized unique_ptrs:

```
1    struct EmployeeFactory
2    {
3      static Contact main;
4      static Contact aux;
5
6      static unique_ptr<Contact> NewMainOfficeEmployee(string
       name, int suite)
7      {
8        return NewEmployee(name, suite, main);
9      }
10
```

```
11    static unique_ptr<Contact> NewAuxOfficeEmployee(string
      name, int suite)
12    {
13      return NewEmployee(name, suite, aux);
14    }
15
16  private:
17    static unique_ptr<Contact> NewEmployee(
18      string name, int suite, Contact& proto)
19    {
20      auto result = make_unique<Contact>(proto);
21      result->name = name;
22      result->address->suite = suite;
23      return result;
24    }
25  };
```

The preceding could now be used as follows:

```
1  auto john = EmployeeFactory::NewAuxOfficeEmployee("John
   Doe", 123);
2  auto jane = EmployeeFactory::NewMainOfficeEmployee("Jane
   Doe", 125);
```

Why use a factory? Well, consider the situation where we copy a prototype and then *forget* to customize it. It will have some blank strings and zeros where actual data should be. Using the approaches from our discussion of Factories, we can, for example, make all non-fully initializing constructors private, declare EmployeeFactory as a friend class, and there you go—now the client has no way of getting a partially constructed Contact.

Summary

The Prototype design pattern embodies the notion of *deep* copying of objects so that, instead of doing full initialization each time, you can take a premade object, copy it, fiddle it a little bit, and then use it independently of the original.

There are really only two ways of implementing the Prototype pattern in C++, and both of them require manual manipulation. They are:

- Writing code that correctly duplicates your object, that is, performs a deep copy. This can be done in a copy constructor/copy assignment operator or in a separate member function.

- Write code for the support of serialization/deserialization and then use this mechanism to implement cloning as serialization immediately followed by deserialization. This carries the extra computational cost; its significance depends on how often you need to do the copying. The *only* advantage of this approach, compared with using, say, copy constructors, is that you get serialization for free.

Whichever approach you choose, some work will be required. Code generation tools (e.g., ReSharper, CLion) can help here if you decide to choose either of these two approaches. Finally, don't forget that if you store data by value, you don't really have a problem.

CHAPTER 5

Singleton

The Singleton is the most hated design pattern in the (rather limited) history of design patterns. Just stating that, however, doesn't mean you shouldn't use the singleton: a toilet brush is not the most pleasant device either, but sometimes it's simply necessary.

The Singleton design pattern grew out of a very simple idea that you should only have one instance of a particular component in your application. For example, a component that loads a database into memory and offers a read-only interface is a prime candidate for a Singleton, since it really doesn't make sense to waste memory storing several identical datasets. In fact, your application might have constraints such that two or more instances of the database simply won't fit into memory, or will result in such a lack of memory as to cause the program to malfunction.

Singleton as Global Object

The naïve approach to this problem is to simply agree that we are not going to instantiate this object ever, for example:

```
1   struct Database
2   {
3     /**
4      * \brief Please do not create more than one instance.
5      */
6     Database() {}
7   };
```

© Dmitri Nesteruk 2018
D. Nesteruk, *Design Patterns in Modern C++*, https://doi.org/10.1007/978-1-4842-3603-1_5

Now, the problem with this approach, apart from the fact that your developer colleagues might simply ignore the advice, is that objects can be created in stealthy ways where the call to the constructor isn't immediately obvious. This can be anything—copy constructor/assignment, a make_unique() call, or the use of an inversion of control (IoC) container.

The most obvious idea that comes to mind is to offer a single, static global object:

```
1   static Database database{};
```

The trouble with global static objects is that their initialization order in different compilation units is undefined. This can lead to nasty effects, like one global object referring to another when the latter hasn't yet been initialized. There's also the issue of discoverability: how does the client know that a global variable exists? Discovering classes is somewhat easier becaue **Go to Type** gives a much more reduced set then autocompletion after : :.

One way to mitigate this is to offer a global (or indeed, member) *function* that exposes the necessary object:

```
1   Database& get_database()
2   {
3       static Database database;
4       return database;
5   }
```

This function can be called to get a reference to the database. You should be aware, however, that thread safety for the preceding is only guaranteed since C++11, and you should check whether your compiler is actually prepated to insert locks to prevent concurrent access while the static object is initializing.

Of course, it's very easy for this scenario to go pear shaped: if Database decides to use some other, similarly exposed, singleton in its destructor, the program is likely to blow up. This raises more of a philosophical point: is it OK for singletons to refer to other singletons?

Classic Implementation

One aspect of the preceding implementations that has been completely neglected is the prevention of the construction of additional objects. Having a global static Database doesn't really prevent anyone from making another instance.

We can easily turn life sour for those interested in making more than one instance of an object: simply put a static counter right in the constructor and throw if the value is ever incremented:

```
1   struct Database
2   {
3     Database()
4     {
5       static int instance_count{ 0 };
6       if (++instance_count > 1)
7         throw std::exception("Cannot make >1 database!");
8     }
9   };
```

This is a particularly hostile approach to the problem: even though it prevents the creation of more than one instance by throwing an exception, it fails to *communicate* the fact that we don't want anyone calling the constructor more than once.

The only way to prevent explicit construction of Database is to once again make its constructor private and introduce the aforementioned function as a *member* function to return the one and only instance:

```
1   struct Database
2   {
3   protected:
4     Database() { /* do what you need to do */ }
5   public:
6     static Database& get()
```

77

```
 7    {
 8        // thread-safe in C++11
 9        static Database database;
10        return database;
11    }
12    Database(Database const&) = delete;
13    Database(Database&&) = delete;
14    Database& operator=(Database const&) = delete;
15    Database& operator=(Database &&) = delete;
16  };
```

Note how we completely removed any possibility of creating Database instances by hiding the constructor and deleting copy/move constructor/ assignment operators.

In pre-C++11 days, you would simply make the copy constructor/assignment private to achieve roughly the same purpose. As an alternative to doing this by hand, you might want to check out boost::noncopyable, a class that you can inherit that adds roughly the same definitions in terms of hiding the members... except it doesn't affect move constructor/assignment.

I reiterate, once again, that if database depends on other static or global variables, using them in its destructor is not safe, as destruction order for these objects is not deterministic, and you might actually be calling objects that have already been destroyed.

Finally, in a particularly nasty trick, you can impletment get() as a heap allocation (so that only the pointer, not the entire object, is static).

```
1  static Database& get() {
2      static Database* database = new Database();
3      return *database;
4  }
```

The preceding implementation relies on the assumption that Database lives until the end of the program and the use of a pointer instead of a reference ensures that a destructor, even if you make one (which, if you do, would have to be public), is never called. And no, the preceding code doesn't cause a memory leak.

Thread Safety

As I've already mentioned, initialization of a singleton in the manner listed previously is thread safe since C++11, meaning that if two threads were to simultaneously call get(), we wouldn't run into a situation where the database would be created twice.

Prior to C++11, you would construct the singleton using an approach called *double-checked locking*. A typical implementation would look like this:

```
1   struct Database
2   {
3     // same members as before, but then...
4     static Database& instance();
5   private:
6     static boost::atomic<Database*> instance;
7     static boost::mutex mtx;
8   };
9
10  Database& Database::instance()
11  {
12    Database* db = instance.load(boost::memory_order_consume);
13    if (!db)
14    {
15      boost::mutex::scoped_lock lock(mtx);
16      db = instance.load(boost::memory_order_consume);
17      if (!db)
```

```
18        {
19            db = new Database();
20            instance.store(db, boost::memory_order_release);
21        }
22     }
23   }
```

Since this book is concerned with Modern C++, we won't dwell on this approach any further.

The Trouble with Singleton

Let's suppose that our database contains a list of capital cities and their populations. The interface that our singleton database is going to conform to is:

```
1   class Database
2   {
3   public:
4     virtual int get_population(const std::string& name) = 0;
5   };
```

We have a single member function that gets us the population for a given city. Now, let us suppose that this interface is adopted by a concrete implementation called SingletonDatabase that implements the singleton the same way as we've done before:

```
1   class SingletonDatabase : public Database
2   {
3     SingletonDatabase() { /* read data from database */ }
4     std::map<std::string, int> capitals;
5   public:
6     SingletonDatabase(SingletonDatabase const&) = delete;
```

```
 7      void operator=(SingletonDatabase const&) = delete;
 8
 9      static SingletonDatabase& get()
10      {
11        static SingletonDatabase db;
12        return db;
13      }
14
15      int get_population(const std::string& name) override
16      {
17        return capitals[name];
18      }
19    };
```

As we noted, the real problem with singletons like the preceding one is their use in other components. Here's what I mean: suppose that, on the basis of the preceding example, we build a component for calculating the sum total population of several different cities:

```
 1    struct SingletonRecordFinder
 2    {
 3      int total_population(std::vector<std::string> names)
 4      {
 5        int result = 0;
 6        for (auto& name : names)
 7          result += SingletonDatabase::get().
            get_population(name);
 8        return result;
 9      }
10    };
```

The trouble is that SingletonRecordFinder is now firmly dependent on SingletonDatabase. This presents an issue for testing: if we want to check that SingletonRecordFinder works correctly, we need to use data from the actual database, that is:

```
1   TEST(RecordFinderTests, SingletonTotalPopulationTest)
2   {
3     SingletonRecordFinder rf;
4     std::vector<std::string> names{ "Seoul", "Mexico City" };
5     int tp = rf.total_population(names);
6     EXPECT_EQ(17500000 + 17400000, tp);
7   }
```

But what if we don't want to use an actual database for a test? What if we want to use some other dummy component instead? Well, in our current design, this is impossible, and it is precisely this inflexibility that is the Singeton's downfall.

So, what can we do? Well, for one, we need to stop depending on Singleton-Database explicitly. Since all we need is something implementing the Database interface, we can create a new ConfigurableRecordFinder that lets us configure where the data comes from:

```
1   struct ConfigurableRecordFinder
2   {
3     explicit ConfigurableRecordFinder(Database& db)
4       : db{db} {}
5
6     int total_population(std::vector<std::string> names)
7     {
8       int result = 0;
9       for (auto& name : names)
10        result += db.get_population(name);
11      return result;
```

```
12      }
13
14      Database& db;
15    };
```

We now use the db reference instead of using the singleton explicitly.
This lets us make a dummy database specifically for testing the record finder:

```
1     class DummyDatabase : public Database
2     {
3       std::map<std::string, int> capitals;
4     public:
5       DummyDatabase()
6       {
7         capitals["alpha"] = 1;
8         capitals["beta"] = 2;
9         capitals["gamma"] = 3;
10      }
11
12      int get_population(const std::string& name) override {
13        return capitals[name];
14      }
15    };
```

And now, we can rewrite our unit test to take advantage of this
DummyDatabase:

```
1     TEST(RecordFinderTests, DummyTotalPopulationTest)
2     {
3       DummyDatabase db{};
4       ConfigurableRecordFinder rf{ db };
5       EXPECT_EQ(4, rf.total_population(
6         std::vector<std::string>{"alpha", "gamma"}));
7     }
```

This test is more robust because if data changes in the actual database, we won't have to adjust our unit test values—the dummy data stays the same.

Singletons and Inversion of Control

The approach with explicitly making a component a singleton is distinctly invasive, and a decision to stop treating the class as a Singleton down the line will end up particularly costly. An alternative solution is to adopt a convention where, instead of directly enforcing the lifetime of a class, this function is outsourced to an IoC container.

Here's what defining a singleton component looks like when using the Boost.DI dependency injection framework:

```
1   auto injector = di::make_injector(
2     di::bind<IFoo>.to<Foo>.in(di::singleton),
3     // other configuration steps here
4   );
```

In the preceding, I use the first letter I in a type name to indicate an interface type. Essentially, what the di::bind line says is that, whenever we need a component that has a member of type IFoo, we initialize that component with a singleton instance of Foo.

According to many people, using a singleton in a DI container is the only socially acceptable use of a singleton. At least with this approach, if you need to replace a singleton object with something else, you can do it in one central place: the container configuration code. An added benefit is that you won't have to implement any singleton logic yourself, which prevents possible errors. Oh, and did I mention that Boost.DI is thread safe?

Monostate

Monostate is a variation on the Singleton pattern. It is a class that *behaves* like a singleton while appearing as an ordinary class.

```
1   class Printer
2   {
3     static int id;
4   public:
5     int get_id() const { return id; }
6     void set_id(int value) { id = value; }
7   };
```

Can you see what's happening here? The class appears as an ordinary class with getters and setters, but they actually work on `static` data!

This might seem like a really neat trick: you let people instantiate `Printer` but they all refer to the same data. However, how are users supposed to know this? A user will happily instantiate two printers, assign them different `id`s, and be very surprised when both of them are identical!

The Monostate approach works to some degree and has a couple of advantages. For example, it is easy to inherit, it can leverage polymorphism, and its lifetime is reasonbly well defined (but then again, you might not always wish it so). Its greatest advantage is that you can take an existing object that's already used throughout the system, patch it up to behave in a Monostate way, and provided your system works fine with the nonplurality of object intances, you've got yourself a Singleton-like implementation with no extra code needing to be rewritten.

The disadvantages are obvious, too: it is an intrusive approach (converting an ordinary object to a Monostate is not easy), and its use of static members means it *always* takes up space, even when it's not needed. Ultimately, Monostate's greatest downfall is that it makes a very optimistic assumption that the class fields are always exposed through getters and setters. If they are being accessed directly, your refactoring is almost doomed to fail.[1]

Summary

Singletons aren't totally evil but, when used carelessly, they'll mess up the testability and refactorability of your application. If you really must use a singleton, try avoiding using it directly (as in, writing `SomeComponent.getInstance().foo()`) and instead keep specifying it as a dependency (e.g., a constructor argument) where all dependencies are satisfied from a single location in your application (e.g., an inversion of *control* container).

---

[1]To be fair, you *can* have your cake and eat it to, but you will need to use the nonstandard `__declspec(property)` extension to do it.

PART II

Structural Patterns

As the name suggests, Structural patterns are all about setting up the structure of your application so as to improve SOLID conformance as well as general usability and refactorability of your code.

When it comes to determining the structure of an object, we can employ two fairly well-known methods:

- Inheritance: an object automatically acquires the nonprivate fields and functions of its base class or classes. To allow instantiation, the object must implement every pure virtual member from its parents; if it does not, it is abstract and cannot be created (but you can inherit from it).

- Composition: generally implies that the child cannot exist without the parent. Think of an object having members of owner<T> type: when the object gets destroyed, they get destroyed with it.

- Aggregation: an object can contain another object, but that object can also exist independently. Think of an object having members of type T* or shared_ptr<T>.

Nowadays, both composition and aggregation are treated in an identical fashion. If you have a `Person` class with a field of type `Address`, you have a choice as to whether `Address` is an external type or a nested type. In either case, provided it's `public`, you can instantiate it as either `Address` or `Person::Address`.

I would argue that using the word *composition* when we really mean aggregation has become so commonplace that we may as well use them in interchangeable fashion. Here's some proof: when we talk about IoC containers, we speak of a *composition root*. But wait, doesn't the IoC container control the lifetime of each object individually? It does, and so we're using the word "composition" when we really mean "aggregation" here.

CHAPTER 6

Adapter

I used to travel quite a lot, and a travel adapter that lets me plug a European plug into a UK or USA socket[1] is a very good analogy to what's going on with the Adapter pattern: we are given an interface, but we want a different one, and building an adapter over the interface is what gets us to where we want to be.

Scenario

Here's a trivial example: suppose you're working with a library that's great at drawing pixels. You, on the other hand, work with geometric objects—lines, rectangles, that sort of thing. You want to keep working with those objects but also need the rendering, so you need to *adapt* your geometry to pixel-based representation.

Let us begin by defining the (rather simple) domain objects of our example:

```
1   struct Point
2   {
3     int x, y;
4   };
5
```

---

[1]Just in case you're European like me and want to complain that everyone should be using European sockets: *no*; the UK design is technically better and safer, so if we did want just one standard, the UK one would be the one to go for.

© Dmitri Nesteruk 2018
D. Nesteruk, *Design Patterns in Modern C++*, https://doi.org/10.1007/978-1-4842-3603-1_6

```
6    struct Line
7    {
8      Point start, end;
9    };
```

Let's now theorize about vector geometry. A typical vector object is likely to be defined by a collection of Line objects. Instead of inheriting from a vector<Line>, we can just define a pair of pure virtual iterator methods:

```
1    struct VectorObject
2    {
3      virtual std::vector<Line>::iterator begin() = 0;
4      virtual std::vector<Line>::iterator end() = 0;
5    };
```

So this way, if you want to define, say, a Rectangle, you can keep a bunch of lines in a vector<Line>-typed field and simply expose its endpoints:

```
1    struct VectorRectangle : VectorObject
2    {
3      VectorRectangle(int x, int y, int width, int height)
4      {
5        lines.emplace_back(Line{ Point{x,y},
         Point{x + width,y} });
6        lines.emplace_back(Line{ Point{x + width,y},
         Point{x+width, y+height} });
7        lines.emplace_back(Line{ Point{x,y},
         Point{x,y+height} });
8        lines.emplace_back(Line{ Point{ x,y + height },
9        Point{ x + width, y + height } });
10     }
11
```

```
12    std::vector<Line>::iterator begin() override {
13      return lines.begin();
14    }
15    std::vector<Line>::iterator end() override {
16      return lines.end();
17    }
18  private:
19    std::vector<Line> lines;
20  };
```

Now, here's the set-up. Suppose we want to draw lines on screen. Rectangles, even! Unfortunately, we cannot, because the only interface for drawing is literally this:

```
1  void DrawPoints(CPaintDC& dc, std::vector<Point>::iterator\
2  start, std::vector<Point>::iterator end)
3  {
4    for (auto i = start; i != end; ++i)
5      dc.SetPixel(i->x, i->y, 0);
6  }
```

I'm using the CPaintDC class from MFC (Microsoft Foundation Classes) here, but that's beside the point. The point is we need pixels. And we only have lines. We need an adapter.

Adapter

All right, so let's suppose we want to draw a couple of rectangles:

```
1  vector<shared_ptr<VectorObject>> vectorObjects{
2    make_shared<VectorRectangle>(10,10,100,100),
3    make_shared<VectorRectangle>(30,30,60,60)
4  }
```

In order to draw these objects, we need to convert every one of them from a series of lines into a rather large number of points. For this, we make a separate class that will store the points and expose them as a pair of iterators:

```
1   struct LineToPointAdapter
2   {
3     typedef vector<Point> Points;
4
5     LineToPointAdapter(Line& line)
6     {
7       // TODO
8     }
9
10    virtual Points::iterator begin() { return points.
      begin(); }
11    virtual Points::iterator end() { return points.end(); }
12  private:
13    Points points;
14  };
```

The conversion from a line to a number of points happens right in the constructor, so the adapter is *eager*.[2] The actual code for the conversion is also rather simple:

```
1   LineToPointAdapter(Line& line)
2   {
3     int left = min(line.start.x, line.end.x);
```

---

[2]Could we have made the adapter lazy? Sure, we could just save the line locally (because it's a reference and we don't want it to go stale or change) and then, whenever someone called begin(), perform initialization if it hasn't been done already. However, if we had *several* adapter members, this init check would have to be repeated in every single member.

```
4      int right = max(line.start.x, line.end.x);
5      int top = min(line.start.y, line.end.y);
6      int bottom = max(line.start.y, line.end.y);
7      int dx = right - left;
8      int dy = line.end.y - line.start.y;
9
10     // only vertical or horizontal lines
11     if (dx == 0)
12     {
13       // vertical
14       for (int y = top; y <= bottom; ++y)
15       {
16         points.emplace_back(Point{ left,y });
17       }
18     }
19     else if (dy == 0)
20     {
21       for (int x = left; x <= right; ++x)
22       {
23         points.emplace_back(Point{ x, top });
24       }
25     }
26   }
```

The preceding code above trivial: we only handle perfectly vertical or horizontal lines and ignore everything else. We can now use this adapter to actually render some objects. We take the two rectangles from the examplee and simply render them like this:

```
1    for (auto& obj : vectorObjects)
2    {
3      for (auto& line : *obj)
4      {
```

```
5        LineToPointAdapter lpo{ line };
6        DrawPoints(dc, lpo.begin(), lpo.end());
7    }
8  }
```

Beautiful! All we do is, for every vector object, get each of its lines, construct a `LineToPointAdapter` for that line, and then iterate the set of points produced by the adapter, feeding them to `DrawPoints()`. And it works! (Trust me, it does.)

Adapter Temporaries

There's a major problem with our code, though: `DrawPoints()` gets called on literally every screen refresh that we might need, which means the same data for same line objects gets regenerated by the adapter, like, a zillion times. What can we do about it?

Well, on the one hand, we can predefine all the points at application start-up, for example:

```
1   vector<Point> points;
2   for (auto& o : vectorObjects)
3   {
4     for (auto& l : *o)
5     {
6       LineToPointAdapter lpo{ l };
7       for (auto& p : lpo)
8         points.push_back(p);
9     }
10  }
```

and then the implementation of `DrawPoints()` simplifies to

```
1   DrawPoints(dc, points.begin(), points.end());
```

But let's suppose, for a moment, that the original set of vectorObjects can change. Caching those points makes no sense then, but we still want to avoid the incessant regeneration of potentially repeating data. How do we deal with this? With caching, of course!

First of all, to avoid regeneration, we need unique ways of identifying lines, which transitively means we need unique ways of identifying points. ReSharper's **Generate | Hash function** to the rescue:

```
1    struct Point
2    {
3      int x, y;
4
5      friend std::size_t hash_value(const Point& obj)
6      {
7        std::size_t seed = 0x725C686F;
8        boost::hash_combine(seed, obj.x);
9        boost::hash_combine(seed, obj.y);
10       return seed;
11     }
12   };
13
14   struct Line
15   {
16     Point start, end;
17
18     friend std::size_t hash_value(const Line& obj)
19     {
20       std::size_t seed = 0x719E6B16;
21       boost::hash_combine(seed, obj.start);
22       boost::hash_combine(seed, obj.end);
23       return seed;
24     }
25   };
```

In the preceding example, I've opted for Boost's hash implementation. Now, we can build a new LineToPointCachingAdapter such that it caches the points and regenerates them only when necessary. The implementation is almost the same except for the following nuances.

First, the adapter now has a cache:

```
1    static map<size_t, Points> cache;
```

The type size_t here is precisely the type returned from Boost's hash functions. Now, when it comes to iterating the points generated, we yield them as follows:

```
1    virtual Points::iterator begin() { return cache[line_hash].
     begin(); }
2    virtual Points::iterator end() { return cache[line_hash].
     end(); }
```

And here is the fun part of the algorithm: before generating the points we check whether they've been generated already. If they have, we just exit; if they haven't, we generate them and add them to the cache:

```
1    LineToPointCachingAdapter(Line& line)
2    {
3      static boost::hash<Line> hash;
4      line_hash = hash(line); // note: line_hash is a field!
5      if (cache.find(line_hash) != cache.end())
6        return; // we already have it
7
8      Points points;
9
10     // same code as before
11
12     cache[line_hash] = points;
13   }
```

Yay! Thanks to hash functions and caching, we've drastically cut down on the number of conversions being made. The only problem that remains is the removal of old points after they are no longer needed. This challenging problem is left as an exercise to the reader.

Summary

Adapter is a very simple concept: it allows you to adapt the interface you have to the interface you need. The only real issue with adapters is that, in the process of adaptation, you sometimes end up generating temporary data so as to satisfy some other representation of data. And when this happens, turn to caching: ensuring that new data is only generated when necessary. Oh, and you'll need to do a bit more work if you want to clean up stale data when the cached objects have changed.

Another concern that we haven't really addressed is *laziness*: the current adapter implementation performs the conversion as soon as it is created. What if you only want the work to be done when the adapter is actually *used*? This is rather easy to do and is left as an exercise for the reader.

CHAPTER 7

Bridge

If you've been paying attention to the latest advances in C++ compilers (GCC, Clang, and MSVC, in particular), you might have noticed that compilation speeds are improving. In particular, compilers are getting more and more *incremental*, so that instead of rebuilding the entire translation unit, the compiler can actually only rebuild the definitions that have changed, and reuse the rest.

The reason I'm bringing up C++ compilation is because "one weird trick" (that phrase again!) has been consistently used by developers to try and optimize the speed of compilation in the past.

I am, of course, talking about…

The Pimpl Idiom

Let me first explain the technical side of what happens in the Pimpl idiom. Suppose you decide to make a `Person` class that stores a person's name and allows them to print a greeting. Instead of defining `Person`'s members as you normally would, you proceed to define the class like so:

```
1   struct Person
2   {
3     std::string name;
4     void greet();
5
6     Person();
```

```
7      ~Person();
8
9      class PersonImpl;
10     PersonImpl *impl; // good place for gsl::owner<T>
11   };
```

Well, this is weird. Seems an awful lot of work for a simple class. Let's see... we have the name and the greet() function, but why bother with the constructor and destructor? And what's this class PersonImpl?

What you're looking at is a class that chooses to hide its implementation in yet another class, helpfully called PersonImpl. It is critical to note that this class is *not* defined in the header file, but rather resides in the .cpp file (Person.cpp, so Person and PersonImpl are colocated). Its definition is as simple as

```
1    struct Person::PersonImpl
2    {
3      void greet(Person* p);
4    }
```

The original Person class forward-declares PersonImpl and proceeds to keep a pointer to it. It is precisely this pointer that gets initialized in Person's constructor and gets destroyed in the destructor; feel free to use smart pointers if it makes you feel better.

```
1    Person::Person()
2      : impl(new PersonImpl) {}
3
4    Person::~Person() { delete impl; }
```

And now, we get to implement Person::greet() which, as you may have guessed, just passes control onto PersonImpl::greet():

```
1    void Person::greet()
2    {
```

```
3     impl->greet(this);
4   }
5
6   void Person::PersonImpl::greet(Person* p)
7   {
8     printf("hello %s", p->name.c_str());
9   }
```

So… that's the Pimpl idiom in a nutshell, so the only question is *why?!?* Why bother jumping through all the hoops, delegating greet() and passing a this pointer? There are three advantages to this approach:

- A larger proportion of the class implementation is actually hidden. If your Person class required a rich API full of private/protected members, you'd be exposing all those details to your clients, even if they could never access those members due to private/protected access modifiers. With Pimpl, they can only be given the public interface.

- Modifying the data members of the hidden Impl class does not affect binary compatibility.

- The header file only needs to include the header files needed for the declaration, not the implementation. For example, if Person requires a private member of type vector<string>, you would be forced to #include both <vector> and <string> in the Person.h header (and this is transitive, so anyone using Person.h would be including them too). With the Pimpl idiom, this can be done in the .cpp file instead.

You'll notice that the aforementioned points allow us to preserve a clean, nonchanging header file. A side effect of this is reduced compilation speed. And, what's important for us, Pimpl is actually a good illustration of the Bridge pattern: in our case, the `pimpl` *opaque pointer* (opaque is opposite of transparent, i.e., you have no idea what's behind it) acts as a bridge, gluing the members of a public interface with their underlying implementation that's hidden away in the `.cpp` file.

Bridge

The Pimpl idiom is a very specific illustration of the Bridge design pattern, so let's take a look at something more general. Suppose we have two classes (in the mathematical sense) of objects: geometric shapes and the renderers that can draw them on the screen.

Just as with our illustration of the Adapter pattern, we'll assume that rendering can happen in vector and raster form (though we won't be writing any actual drawing code here) and, in terms of shapes, let's restrict ourselves to just circles.

First of all, here is the `Renderer` base class:

```
1   struct Renderer
2   {
3     virtual void render_circle(float x, float y, float
      radius) = 0;
4   };
```

We can construct vector and raster implementations easily; I'll just emulate actual rendering below with some code to write things to the console:

```
1   struct VectorRenderer : Renderer
2   {
3     void render_circle(float x, float y, float radius) override
```

```
4    {
5        cout << "Rasterizing circle of radius " << radius <<
         endl;
6      }
7    };
8
9    struct RasterRenderer : Renderer
10   {
11     void render_circle(float x, float y, float radius)
       override
12     {
13         cout << "Drawing a vector circle of radius " << radius
           << endl;
14     }
15   };
```

The base class Shape will keep a reference to the renderer; the shape will support self-rendering with the draw() member function, and will also support the resize() operation:

```
1    struct Shape
2    {
3    protected:
4      Renderer& renderer;
5      Shape(Renderer& renderer) : renderer{ renderer } {}
6    public:
7      virtual void draw() = 0;
8      virtual void resize(float factor) = 0;
9    };
```

You'll notice that the Shape class makes a reference to a Renderer. This happens to be the bridge that we build. We can now create an implementation of the Shape class, supplying additional information such as the position of the circle's center as well as the radius.

```
1    struct Circle : Shape
2    {
3      float x, y, radius;
4
5      void draw() override
6      {
7        renderer.render_circle(x, y, radius);
8      }
9
10     void resize(float factor) override
11     {
12       radius *= factor;
13     }
14
15     Circle(Renderer& renderer, float x, float y, float radius)
16       : Shape{renderer}, x{x}, y{y}, radius{radius} {}
17   };
```

OK, so this pattern is exposed rather quickly, and the interesting part is, of course, in draw(): that's where we use the bridge to connect the Circle (which has information about its location and size) to the process of rendering. And the exact thing that is the bridge here is a Renderer, for example:

```
1    RasterRenderer rr;
2    Circle raster_circle{ rr, 5,5,5 };
3    raster_circle.draw();
4    raster_circle.resize(2);
5    raster_circle.draw();
```

In the preceding case, the bridge is the `RasterRenderer`: you make it, pass a reference into `Circle` and from then on, calls to `draw()` would use this `RasterRenderer` as the bridge, drawing the circle. If you need to fine-tune the circle, you can `resize()` it, and the rendering will still work just fine, as the renderer doesn't know or care about the `Circle` and doesn't even take it as reference!

Summary

The Bridge is a rather simple concept, serving as a connector or glue, connecting two pieces together. The use of abstraction (interfaces) allows components to interact with one another without really being aware of the concrete implementations.

That said, the participants of the Bridge pattern do need to be aware of each other's existence. Specifically, a `Circle` needs a reference to the `Renderer` and, conversely, the `Renderer` knows how to specifically draw circles (thus, the name of the `draw_circle()` member function). This can be contrasted with the Mediator pattern, which allows objects to communicate without being directly aware of each other.

CHAPTER 8

Composite

It's a fact of life that objects are quite often composed of other objects (or, in other words, they aggregate other objects). Remember, we agreed to equate aggregation and composition at the start of this part of the book.

There are very few ways for an object to advertise that it's composed of something. Fields, by themselves, do not constitute an interface unless you make virtual getters and setters. You *can* advertise being composed of a collection of objects by implementing begin()/end() members, but keep in mind that this doesn't actually state a lot: after all, you can do *anything* you want in it. Similarly, you can try to advertise that you are a containiner of a *specific* type by doing an iterator typedef, but is anyone really going to check it?

Another option for advertising being a container is inheriting from a container. This is *mostly* fine: even though STL containers do not have virtual destructors, if *you* don't need anything in your destructor either, and you don't envisage people inheriting from *your* type, then everything is fine—go ahead and inherit from std::vector; nothing bad should happen.

So, what is the Composite pattern about? Essentially, we try to give single objects and groups of objects an identical interface. And sure, it's easy to just define an interface and implement it in both objects. But equally you can try leveraging duck typing mechanisms such as begin()/end()

© Dmitri Nesteruk 2018
D. Nesteruk, *Design Patterns in Modern C++*, https://doi.org/10.1007/978-1-4842-3603-1_8

where applicable.[1] Duck typing, in general, is a *terrible idea* because it relies on secret knowledge instead of being explicitly defined in an interface somewhere. By the way, nothing prevents you from making an explicit interface with begin() and end(), but what is the iterator type?

Array Backed Properties

The Composite design pattern is typically applied to entire classes but, before we get to that, I want to show you how it can be used on the scale of properties. By the term *property*, I am of course referring to the class' fields as well as the way those fields are exposed to the API consumer.

Imagine a computer game with creatures that have different numeric traits. Each creature can have a strength value, an agility value, and so on. So this is very easy to define:

```
1    class Creature
2    {
3      int strength, agility, intelligence;
4    public:
5      int get_strength() const
6      {
7        return strength;
8      }
9
10     void set_strength(int strength)
11     {
12       Creature::strength = strength;
13     }
```

---

[1]To be fair, the begin()/end() duopoly is excessive; we could take a cue from Swift and define an interface with a single member such as: std::optional<T> next(). This way, you can just call next() until it gives you an empty value. Writing something like while (auto item = foo.next()) { ... }

```
14      // other getter and setters here
15    };
```

So far, so good. But now imagine we want to calculate some aggregate statistics on the creature. For example, we want to know the sum of its statistics, the average value accross all statistics as well as, say, the highest value. Since our data is fragmented into fields, we end up with the following implementation:

```
1    class Creature
2    {
3      // other members here
4      int sum() const {
5        return strength + agility + intelligence;
6      }
7
8      double average() const {
9        return sum() / 3.0;
10     }
11
12     int max() const {
13       return ::max(::max(strength, agility), intelligence);
14     }
15   };
```

This implementation is unpleasant for a number of reasons:

- When calculating the sum of all statistics, we could easily make a mistake and forget one of them.

- When calculating the average, we're using a bona fide *magic number* 3.0 that corresponds to the number of fields that are used in the calculation.

- When calculating the maximum, we have to construct pairs-of-pairs of std::max() calls.

The code is terrible as-is; now imagine adding another property to the mix. This would require truly awful refactoring of sum(), average(), max(), and any other aggregate calculation. Can this be avoided? Well, it turns out it can.

The approach of using *array-backed properties* is as follows. First of all, we define enumeration members for all the required properties, and then proceed to create an array of the appropriate size:

```
1   class Creature
2   {
3     enum Abilities { str, agl, intl, count };
4     array<int, count> abilities;
5   };
```

The above enum definition has an extra value called count that tells us how many elements we have in total. Note that we are using an enum, not an enum class, which makes the use of those members a little bit easier.

We can now define getters and setters for strength, agility, etc. being projected into our backing array, for example:

```
1   int get_strength() const { return abilities[str]; }
2   void set_strength(int value) { abilities[str] = value; }
3   // same for other properties
```

This is the kind of code that your IDE will *not* generate for you, but that's a small price to pay for the flexibility.

Now, here come the awesome parts: our calculations of sum(), average(), and max() become truly trivial because, in all of those cases, all we have to do is iterate an array:

```
1   int sum() const {
2     return accumulate(abilities.begin(), abilities.end(), 0);
3   }
4
```

```
5    double average() const {
6      return sum() / (double)count;
7    }
8
9    int max() const {
10     return *max_element(abilities.begin(), abilities.end());
11   }
```

Isn't this great? Not only is the code a lot easier to write and maintain, but adding a new property to the class is as simple as adding a new enum member and a getter-setter pair; the aggregates need not change at all!

Grouping Graphic Objects

Think of an application such as PowerPoint where you can select several different objects and drag them as one. And yet, if you were to select a single object, you can grab that object too. Same goes for rendering: you can render an individual graphic object, or you can group several shapes together and they get drawn as one group.

The implementation of this approach is rather easy because it relies on just a single interface such as the following:

```
1    struct GraphicObject
2    {
3      virtual void draw() = 0;
4    };
```

Now, from the name, you could be forgiven for thinking that a GraphicObject is always scalar, that is, it always represents a single item. However, think about it: several rectangles and circles grouped together represent a Composite graphic object (hence the name of the Composite design pattern). So just as I can define, say, a circle:

```
1   struct Circle : GraphicObject
2   {
3     void draw() override
4     {
5       std::cout << "Circle" << std::endl;
6     }
7   };
```

in a similar vein, I can define a GraphicObject that is made up of several other graphic objects. Yes, the relationship can be infinitely recursive:

```
1   struct Group : GraphicObject
2   {
3     std::string name;
4
5     explicit Group(const std::string& name)
6       : name{name} {}
7
8     void draw() override
9     {
10      std::cout << "Group " << name.c_str() << " contains:"
        << std::endl;
11      for (auto&& o : objects)
12        o->draw();
13    }
14
15    std::vector<GraphicObject*> objects;
16  };
```

Both a scalar `Circle` and any `Group` are drawable insofar as they both implement the draw() function. `Group` keeps a vector of pointers to other graphic objects (those can be `Groups` too!) and uses that vector for rendering itself.

Here's how this API can be used:

```
1    Group root("root");
2    Circle c1, c2;
3    root.objects.push_back(&c1);
4
5    Group subgroup("sub");
6    subgroup.objects.push_back(&c2);
7
8    root.objects.push_back(&subgroup);
9
10   root.draw();
```

The preceding generates the following output:

```
1    Group root contains:
2    Circle
3    Group sub contains:
4    Circle
```

And this is the simplest implementation of the Composite design pattern, albeit with a custom interface that we ourselves have defined. Now, how would this pattern look if we tried to adopt the approach of some of the other, more standardized ways of iterating objects?

Neural Networks

Machine Learning is the hot new thing, and I hope it stays this way or I'll have to update this paragraph. Part of machine learning is the use of artificial neural networks: software constructs that attempt to mimic the way neurons work in our brains.

The central concept of neural networks is, of course, a *neuron*. A neuron can produce a (typically numeric) output as a function of its inputs, and we can feed that value on to other connections in the network. We're going to concern ourselves with connections only, so we'll model the neuron thus:

```
1   struct Neuron
2   {
3     vector<Neuron*> in, out;
4     unsigned int id;
5
6     Neuron()
7     {
8       static int id = 1;
9       this->id = id++;
10    }
11  };
```

I've thrown in the id field for identification. Now, what you probably want to do is to be able to connect one neuron to another, which can be done using

```
1   template<> void connect_to<Neuron>(Neuron& other)
2   {
3     out.push_back(&other);
4     other.in.push_back(this);
5   }
```

This function does fairly predictable things: it sets up connections between the current (this) neuron and some other one. So far, so good.

Now, suppose we also want to create neuron *layers*. A layer is quite simply a specific number of neurons grouped together. Let us once again commit the cardinal sin of inheriting from std::vector:

```
1  struct NeuronLayer : vector<Neuron>
2  {
3    NeuronLayer(int count)
4    {
5      while (count --> 0)
6        emplace_back(Neuron{});
7    }
8  };
```

Looks good, right? I've even thrown in operator --> for you to enjoy.[2] But now, we've got a bit of a problem.

The problem is this: we want to be able to have neurons connectable to neuron layers. Broadly speaking, we want this to work:

```
1  Neuron n1, n2;
2  NeuronLayer layer1, layer2;
3  n1.connect_to(n2);
4  n1.connect_to(layer1);
5  layer1.connect_to(n1);
6  layer1.connect_to(layer2);
```

---

[2]There is, of course, no --> operator; it's quite simply the postfix decrement– followed by greater-than >. The effect, though, is exactly as the --> arrow suggests: in while (count --> 0) we iterate until count reaches zero. You can do similar tricks with "operators" such as <--, --->, et cetera.

As you can see, we've got four distinct cases to take care of:

1. Neuron connecting to another neuron

2. Neuron connecting to layer

3. Layer connecting to neuron; and

4. Layer connecting to another layer

As you may have guessed, there's no way in Baator that we'll be making four overloads of the connect_to() member function. What if there were three distinct classes—would you realistically consider creating nine functions? I do not think so.

Instead, what we are going to do is slot in a base class—we can totally do that, thanks to multiple inheritance. So, how about the following?

```
1   template <typename Self>
2   struct SomeNeurons
3   {
4     template <typename T> void connect_to(T& other)
5     {
6       for (Neuron& from : *static_cast<Self*>(this))
7       {
8         for (Neuron& to : other)
9         {
10          from.out.push_back(&to);
11          to.in.push_back(&from);
12        }
13      }
14    }
15  };
```

The implementation of connect_to() is definitely worth discussing. As you can see, it's a template member function that takes T and then proceeds to iterate *this and T&'s neurons pairwise, interconnecting each pair. But there is a caveat: we cannot just iterate *this, since this will give us a SomeNeurons& and what we're after is the actual type.

This is why we are forced to make SomeNeurons& become a template class, where the template argument Self refers to the inheritor class. We then proceed to cast the this pointer to Self* before dereferencing it and iterating the contents. This implies that Neuron must inherit from SomeNeurons<Neuron>—a small price to pay for the convenience.

All that is left is to implement SomeNeurons::begin() and end() in both Neuron and NeuronLayer for the range-based for loops to actually work.

Since NeuronLayer inherits from vector<Neuron>, explicit implementation of the begin()/end() pairs is not required—it's automatically present there already. But the Neuron does need a way to iterate... itself, basically. It needs to yield itself as the only iterable element. This can be done as follows:

```
1  Neuron* begin() override { return this; }
2  Neuron* end() override { return this + 1; }
```

I'll give you a moment or two to appreciate the fiendishness of this design. It is precisely this piece of magic that makes SomeNeurons::connect_to() possible. In short, we've made a singular (scalar) object behave like an iterable collection of objects. This allows all of the following uses:

```
1  Neuron neuron, neuron2;
2  NeuronLayer layer, layer2;
3
4  neuron.connect_to(neuron2);
5  neuron.connect_to(layer);
6  layer.connect_to(neuron);
7  layer.connect_to(layer2);
```

Not to mention the fact that, if you were to introduce a new container (say, some NeuronRing), all you would have to do is inherit from SomeNeurons<NeuronRing>, implement begin()/end(), and the new class will be immediately connectable to all Neurons and NeuronLayers.

Summary

The Composite design pattern allows us to provide identical interfaces for individual objects and collections of objects. This can be done either through the explicit use of interface members or, alternatively, through *duck typing*—for example, range-based for loops don't require you to inherit anything, and work on the basis of the typing having suitable-looking begin()/end() members.

It is precisely these begin()/end() members that allow a scalar type to masquerade as a "collection." It is also interesting to note that the nested for loops of our connect_to() function are able to connect the two constructs together despite them having *different* iterator types: Neuron returns a Neuron* whereas NeuronLayer returns vector<Neuron>::iterator—these two are not quite the same thing. Ahh, the magic of templates!

Finally, I must admit that all of these jumps through hoops are necessary only if you want to have a *single member function*. If you are OK with calling a global function or if you are happy with having more than one connect_to() implementation, the base class SomeNeurons is unnecessary.

CHAPTER 9

Decorator

Suppose you're working with a class your colleague wrote, and you want to extend that class' functionality. How would you do it, without modifying the original code? Well, one approach is inheritance: you make a derived class, add the functionality you need, maybe even override something, and you're good to go.

Right, except this doesn't always work, and there are many reasons why. For example, you typically wouldn't want to inherit from, say, std::vector due to its lack of a virtual destructor, or from int (that's just impossible). But the most critical reason why inheritance doesn't work is the scenario where you need *several* enhancements, and you want to keep those enhancements separate because, you know, Single Responsibility Principle.

The Decorator pattern allows us to enhance existing types without either modifying the original types (Open-Closed Principle) or causing an explosion of the number of derived types.

Scenario

Let me explain what I mean by *multiple* enhancements: suppose you have a class called Shape and you make two inheritors called ColoredShape and Transpar-entShape—you also need to take into account the fact that someone will want a ColoredTransparentShape. So we've generated three classes to support two enhancements; if we had three enhancements, we would need seven (7!) distinct classes. And let's not forget that we actually

© Dmitri Nesteruk 2018
D. Nesteruk, *Design Patterns in Modern C++*, https://doi.org/10.1007/978-1-4842-3603-1_9

want different shapes (Square, Circle, etc.)—what base class would those inherit from? With three enhancements and two distinct shapes, the number of classes would jump up to 14. Clearly, this is an unmanageable situation—even if you are using a tool for code generation!

Let's actually write some code for this. Suppose we define an abstract class called Shape:

```
1   struct Shape
2   {
3     virtual string str() const = 0;
4   };
```

In the preceding class, str() is a virtual function we'll use to provide a textual representation of a particular shape.

We can now implement shapes such as Circle or Square with this interface:

```
1   struct Circle : Shape
2   {
3     float radius;
4
5     explicit Circle(const float radius)
6       : radius{radius} {}
7
8     void resize(float factor) { radius *= factor; }
9
10    string str() const override
11    {
12      ostringstream oss;
13      oss << "A circle of radius " << radius;
14      return oss.str();
15    }
16  }; // Square implementation omitted
```

We already know that ordinary inheritance alone does not offer us an efficient way to provide enhancements to shapes, so we must turn to composition—which is the mechanism that the Decorator pattern uses to enhance objects. There are actually two distinct approaches to this, and several other, patterns that we need to discuss:

- *Dynamic composition* allows you to compose something at runtime, typically by passing around references. It allows maximum flexibility, since the composition can happen at runtime in response to, for example, the user's input.

- *Static composition* implies that the object and its enhancements are composed at compile time via the use of templates. This means the exact set of enhancements on an object needs to be known at the moment of compilation, since it cannot be modified later.

If the preceding sounds a bit too cryptic, don't worry—we are going to implement the Decorator in both dynamic and static ways, so all will become clear very soon.

Dynamic Decorator

Suppose we want to enhance shapes with a bit of color. We use composition instead of inheritance to implement a ColoredShape that simply takes a reference to an already-constructed Shape and enhances it:

```
1   struct ColoredShape : Shape
2   {
3     Shape& shape;
4     string color;
5
6     ColoredShape(Shape& shape, const string& color)
```

```
7         : shape{shape}, color{color} {}
8
9       string str() const override
10      {
11        ostringstream oss;
12        oss << shape.str() << " has the color " << color;
13        return oss.str();
14      }
15    };
```

As you can see, ColoredShape is itself a Shape. You would typically use it like this:

```
1    Circle circle{0.5f};
2    ColoredShape redCircle{circle, "red"};
3    cout << redCircle.str();
4    // prints "A circle of radius 0.5 has the color red"
```

If we now want another enhancement that adds transparency to shapes, this is also trivial:

```
1    struct TransparentShape : Shape
2    {
3      Shape& shape;
4      uint8_t transparency;
5
6      TransparentShape(Shape& shape, const uint8_t transparency)
7        : shape{shape}, transparency{transparency} {}
8
9      string str() const override
10     {
11       ostringstream oss;
12       oss << shape.str() << " has "
13          << static_cast<float>(transparency) / 255.f*100.f
```

```
14          << "% transparency";
15      return oss.str();
16     }
17   };
```

We now have an enhancement that takes a transparency value in 0..255 range and reports it as a percentage value. We cannot use the enhancement on its own:

```
1   Square square{3};
2   TransparentShape demiSquare{square, 85};
3   cout << demiSquare.str();
4   // A square with side 3 has 33.333% transparency
```

But the great thing is we can compose both ColoredShape and TransparentShape together to make a shape that has both color and transparency:

```
1   TransparentShape myCircle{
2     ColoredShape{
3       Circle{23}, "green"
4     }, 64
5   };
6   cout << myCircle.str();
7   // A circle of radius 23 has the color green has 25.098%
    transparency
```

See what I did there? I just constructed the whole thing in place. Now, to be fair, one thing you also *can* do that doesn't make much sense is repeat the same decorator once. For example, it doesn't make sense to have a Colored-Shape{ColoredShape{...}} but it *will* work, giving somewhat conflicting results. And if you decide to fight against it with assertions or some OOP magic—well, you can do that, but I wonder how you will handle something like

```
1   ColoredShape{TransparentShape{ColoredShape{...}}}
```

This is much more challenging to detect, and even though it's possible, I would argue it's simply not worth checking. We need to assume *some* sanity on the part of the programmer.

Static Decorator

Did you notice that, when setting up the scenario, I gave Circle a function called resize() that wasn't part of the Shape interface? As you may have guessed, since it's not part of Shape, you really cannot call it from a decorator. Here's what I mean:

```
1   Circle circle{3};
2   ColoredShape redCircle{circle, "red"};
3   redCircle.resize(2); // won't compile!
```

So suppose you don't really care whether you can compose objects at runtime or not, but you really *do* care about being able to access all the fields and member functions of a decorated object. Is it possible to construct such a decorator?

Well, in actual fact, it is, and it's done through templates and inheritance—but not the kind of inheritance that causes a state space explosion. Instead, we shall apply something called Mixin Inheritance, an approach when the class inherits from its own template argument.

So here's the idea—we'll make a new ColoredShape, one that inherits from a template parameter. We have no way of constraining template parameters to be of any particular type, so we'll use a static_assert instead:

```
1   template <typename T> struct ColoredShape : T
2   {
3     static_assert(is_base_of<Shape, T>::value,
4       "Template argument must be a Shape");
5
6     string color;
7
```

```
8      string str() const override
9      {
10       ostringstream oss;
11       oss << T::str() << " has the color " << color;
12       return oss.str();
13     }
14   }; // implementation of TransparentShape<T> omitted
```

Armed with implementations of ColoredShape<T> and TransparentShape<T>, we can now compose them into a colored, transparent shape:

```
1    ColoredShape<TransparentShape<Square>> square{"blue"};
2    square.size = 2;
3    square.transparency = 0.5;
4    cout << square.str();
5    // can call square's own members
6    square.resize(3);
```

Isn't this great? Well, great but not perfect: we seem to have lost the full use of our constructors, so even though we are able to initialize the outermost class, we cannot fully construct a shape with specific size, color, and transparency in a single line of code.

To put the icing (decorations!) on our cake, let's give ColoredShape and TransparentShape forwarding constructors. These constructors will take two arguments: the first will be the argument specific to the current template class, and the second will be a generic parameter pack that we'll forward to our base class. Here's what I mean:

```
1    template <typename T> struct TransparentShape : T
2    {
3      uint8_t transparency;
4
```

```
 5      template<typename...Args>
 6      TransparentShape(const uint8_t transparency, Args ...args)
 7        : T(std::forward<Args>(args)...)
 8        , transparency{ transparency } {}
 9      ...
10    }; // same for ColoredShape
```

Just to reiterate, the preceding constructor can accept any number of arguments, where the first argument gets used to initialize the transparency value and the rest are simply forwarded to the constructor of the base class, whatever that happens to be.

The number of constructors naturally has to be correct, and the program will fail to compile if their number or the types of values are incorrect. If you start adding default constructors to your types, the use of the overall parameter set becomes a lot more flexible, but can also introduce ambiguities and confusion.

Oh, and make sure to never make these contructors explicit or you'll run afoul of C++'s copy-list-initialization rules when composing the decorators together. Now, how about actually using all this goodness?

```
1   ColoredShape2<TransparentShape2<Square>> sq =
    { "red", 51, 5 };
2   cout << sq.str() << endl;
3   // A square with side 5 has 20% transparency has
    the color red
```

Beautiful! This is precisely what we wanted. This completes the implementation of our static decorator. Again, you could enhance it to avoid repetitive types such as ColoredShape<ColoredShape<...>> or cyclic ones such as ColoredShape<TransparentShape<ColoredShape<...>>> but in a static context this feels like a waste of time. Totally doable, though, thanks to various forms of template magic.

Functional Decorator

While the Decorator pattern is typically applied to classes, it can be equally applied to functions. For example, suppose there's a particular operation in your code that's giving you trouble: you want to log all instances when this is called and analyze the statistics in Excel. Well, this can certainly be done just by putting some code before and after the call, that is:

```
1   cout << "Entering function\n";
2   // do the work
3   cout << "Exiting funcion\n";
```

This works just fine, but isn't good in terms of separation of concerns: we really want to store the logging functionality somewhere so that we can reuse it and enhance it as necessary.

There are different approaches on how to do this. One approach is to simply feed the entire unit of work as a lambda to some logging component similar to the following:

```
1    struct Logger
2    {
3      function<void()> func;
4      string name;
5
6      Logger(const function<void()>& func, const string& name)
7        : func{func},
8          name{name}
9      {
10     }
11
12     void operator()() const
13     {
14       cout << "Entering " << name << endl;
15       func();
```

```
16          cout << "Exiting " << name << endl;
17      }
18    };
```

With this approach, you could write the following:

```
1    Logger([]() {cout << "Hello" << endl; }, "HelloFunction")();
2    // output:
3    // Entering HelloFunction
4    // Hello
5    // Exiting HelloFunction
```

There is always an option of passing in the function not as an std::function but as a template argument. This results in a slight variation of the preceding:

```
1    template <typename Func>
2    struct Logger2
3    {
4      Func func;
5      string name;
6
7      Logger2(const Func& func, const string& name)
8        : func{func}, name{name} {}
9
10     void operator()() const
11     {
12       cout << "Entering " << name << endl;
13       func();
14       cout << "Exiting " << name << endl;
15     }
16   };
```

The use of the preceding implementation is exactly the same. We can make a utility function to actually create such a logger:

```
1    template <typename Func> auto make_logger2(Func func,
2      const string& name)
3    {
4      return Logger2<Func>{ func, name }; // () = call now
5    }
```

and then use it like this:

```
1    auto call = make_logger2([]() {cout << "Hello!" << endl; },
     "HelloFunction");
2    call();
```

"What's the point?" you might ask. Well… we now have a capability to create a decorator (with the decorated function inside it) and to call it at the time of our choosing.

Now, here's a challenge for you: what if you wanted to log the invocation of the function add(), defined as follows…

```
1    double add(double a, double b)
2    {
3      cout << a << "+" << b << "=" << (a + b) << endl;
4      return a + b;
5    }
```

but you also wanted to get the return value? Yep, a return value returned from the logger. Not so easy! But certainly not impossible. Let's make yet another incarnation of our logger:

```
1    template <typename R, typename... Args>
2    struct Logger3<R(Args...)>
3    {
4      Logger3(function<R(Args...)> func, const string& name)
```

```
 5        : func{func},
 6            name{name}
 7      {
 8      }
 9
10      R operator() (Args ...args)
11      {
12        cout << "Entering " << name << endl;
13        R result = func(args...);
14        cout << "Exiting " << name << endl;
15        return result;
16      }
17
18      function<R(Args ...)> func;
19      string name;
20    };
```

In the preceding, the template argument R refers to the type of the return value, and Args, well, you've no doubt guessed already. The decorator holds on to the function and calls it when necessary, the only difference is that operator() returns an R, so you don't lose the return value.

We can construct another utility make_ function:

```
1    template <typename R, typename... Args>
2    auto make_logger3(R (*func)(Args...), const string& name)
3    {
4      return Logger3<R(Args...)>(
5          std::function<R(Args...)>(func),
6          name);
7    }
```

And notice how, instead of going for an `std::function`, I've defined the first argument as an ordinary function pointer. We can now use this function to instantiate the logged invocation and use it:

```
1    auto logged_add = make_logger3(add, "Add");
2    auto result = logged_add(2, 3);
```

Of course, make_logger3 can be supplanted with Dependency Injection. The upside of that approach would be an ability to

- Dynamically turn logging on and off by providing a Null Object[1] instead of an actual logger

- Disable the actual invocation of the code being logged (again, by substituting a different logger)

All in all, another useful tool on the developer's toolbelt. I leave the weaving of this approach into Dependency Injection as an exercise for the reader.

Summary

A decorator gives a class additional functionality while adhering to the OCP. Its crucial aspect is *composability*: several decorators can be applied to an object in any order. We've looked at the following types of decorators:

- *Dynamic decorators* can store references (or even store the entire values, if you want!) of the decorated objects and provide dynamic (runtime) composability, at the expense of not being able to access the underlying objects' own members.

---

[1]The *Null Object* is described in Chapter 19 of this book. Essentially, a Null Object is an object that conforms to some interface, but has empty methods, that is, methods that do absolutely nothing. This solves the problem when you *must* supply an object into an API, but you don't want that object to actually do anything.

- *Static decorators* use mixin inheritance (inheriting from template parameter) to compose decorators at compile-time. This loses any sort of runtime flexibility (you cannot recompose objects) but gives you access to the underlying object's members. These objects are also fully initializable through constructor forwarding.

- *Functional decorators* can wrap either blocks of code or particular functions to allow composition of behaviors.

It's worth mentioning that in languages that do *not* allow multiple inheritance, decorators are also used to simulate it by aggregating more than one object and then providing an interface that is the set union of the interfaces of the aggregated objects.

CHAPTER 10

Façade

First of all, let's get the linguistic issue out of the way: that little curve in the letter Ç is called a *cedilla* and the letter itself is pronounced as an S, so the word 'façade' is pronounced as *fah-saad*. The particularly pendantic among you are welcome to use the letter ç in your code, since most compilers treat it just fine.

Right, now, about that pattern...

I've spent a lot of time working in areas of quant finance and algorithmic trading. As you can probably guess, what's required of a good trading terminal is quick delivery of information into a trader's brain: you want things to be rendered as fast as possible, without any lag.

Most financial data (except for the charts) are actually rendered in plain text: white characters on a black screen. This is, in a way, similar to the way the terminal/console/command-line interface works in your own operating system, but there is a subtle difference.

© Dmitri Nesteruk 2018

D. Nesteruk, *Design Patterns in Modern C++*, https://doi.org/10.1007/978-1-4842-3603-1_10

How the Terminal Works

The first part of a terminal window is the *buffer*. This is where the rendered characters are stored. A buffer is a rectangular area of memory, typically a 1D[1] or 2D char or wchar_t array. A buffer can be much larger than the visible area of the terminal window, so it can store some historical output that you can scroll back to.

Typically, a buffer has a pointer (e.g., an integer) specifying the current input line. That way, a full buffer doesn't reallocate all lines; it just overwrites the oldest one.

Then there's the idea of a *viewport*. A viewport renders a part of the particular buffer. A buffer can be huge, so a viewport just takes a rectangular area out of that buffer and renders that. Naturally, the size of the viewport has to be less than or equal to the size of the buffer.

Finally, there's the console (terminal window) itself. The console shows the viewport, allows scrolling up and down, and even accepts user input. The console is, in fact, a façade: a simplified representation of what is a rather complicated set-up behind the scenes.

Typically, most users interact with a single buffer and viewport. It *is*, however, possible to have a console window where you have, say, the area split vertically between two viewports, each having their corresponding buffers. This can be done using utilities such as the screen Linux command.

---

[1]Most buffers are typically one-dimensional. The reason for this is that it's easier to pass a single pointer somewhere than a double pointer, and using an array or vector doesn't make much sense when the size of the structure is deterministic and immutable. Another advantage to the 1D approach is that, when it comes to GPU processing, a system such as CUDA uses up to six dimensions for addressing *anyway*, so after a while, computing a 1D index from an N-dimensional block/grid position becomes second nature.

An Advanced Terminal

One problem with a typical operating system terminal is that it is *extremely slow* if you pipe a lot of data into it. For example, a Windows terminal window (cmd.exe) uses GDI to render the characters, which is completely unnecessary. In a fast-paced trading environment, you want the rendering to be hardware accelerated: characters should be presented as prerendered textures placed on a surface using an API such as OpenGL.[2]

A trading terminal consists of *multiple* buffers and viewports. In a typical setup, different buffers might be getting updated concurrently with data from various exchanges or trading bots, and all of this information needs to be presented on a single screen.

Buffers also provide functionality that is a lot more exciting that just a 1D or 2D linear storage. For example, a TableBuffer might be defined as:

```
1    struct TableBuffer : IBuffer
2    {
3      TableBuffer(vector<TableColumnSpec> spec, int
       totalHeight) { ... }
4
5      struct TableColumnSpec
6      {
7        string header;
8        int width;
9        enum class TableColumnAlignment {
10         Left, Center, Right
11       } alignment;
12     }
13   };
```

---

[2]We also use ASCII, since Unicode is rarely, if ever, required. Having 1 char = 1 byte is a good practice if you don't need to support extra character sets. While not relevant to the discussion at hand, it also *greatly simplifies* the implementation of string processing algorithms on both GPUs and CPUs.

In other words, a buffer can take some specification and build a table (yes, a good old-fashioned ASCII-formatted table!) and present it on screen.

A viewport is in charge of getting data from the buffer. Some of its characteristics include:

- A reference to the buffer it's showing

- Its size

- If the viewport is smaller than the buffer, it needs to specify which part of the buffer it is going to show. This is expressed in absolute x-y coordinates.

- The location of the viewport on the overall console window

- The location of the cursor, assuming this viewport is currently taking user input

Where's the Façade?

The console itself *is* the façade in this particular system. Internally, the console has to manage tonnes of different objects:

```
1   struct Console
2   {
3     vector<Viewport*> viewports;
4     Size charSize, gridSize;
5     ...
6   };
```

Initialization of the console is also, typically, a very nasty affair. However, since it's a Façade, it actually tries to give a really accessible API. This might take a number of sensible parameters to initialize all the guts from

```
1    Console::Console(bool fullscreen, int char_width, int
     char_height,
2      int width, int height, optional<Size> client_size)
3    {
4      // single buffer and viewport created here
5      // linked together and added to appropriate collections
6      // image textures generated
7      // grid size calculated depending on whether we want
       fullscreen mode
8    }
```

Alternatively, one might pack all those arguments into a single object which, again, has some sensible defaults:

```
1    Console::Console(const ConsoleCreationParameters& ccp) {
     ... }
2
3    struct ConsoleCreationParameters
4    {
5      optional<Size> client_size;
6      int character_width{10};
7      int character_height{14};
8      int width{20};
9      int height{30};
10     bool fullscreen{false};
11     bool create_default_view_and_buffer{true};
12   };
```

Summary

The Façade design pattern is a way of putting a simple interface in front of one or more complicated subsystems. In our example, a complicated set-up involving many buffers and viewports can be used directly or, if you just want a simple console with a single buffer and associated viewport, you can get it through a very accessible and intuitive API.

CHAPTER 11

Flyweight

A Flyweight (also sometimes called a *token* or a *cookie*) is a temporary component that acts as a "smart reference" to something. Typically, flyweights are used in situations where you have a very large number of very similar objects, and you want to minimize the amount of memory that is dedicated to storing all these values.

Let's take a look at some scenarios where this pattern becomes relevant.

User Names

Imagine a massively multiplayer online game. I bet you $20 there's more than one user called John Smith—quite simply because it is a popular name. So if we were to store that name over and over (in ASCII), we would be spending 11 bytes for every such user. Instead, we could store the name once and then store a pointer to every user with that name (which is only 8 bytes). That's quite a saving.

It would, perhaps, make even more sense to fragment the name into first and last names: that way, Fitzgerald Smith would be represented by two pointers (16 bytes), pointing to first and last names, respectively. In fact, we can cut down the number of bytes used drastically if we use indices instead of names. You don't expect there to be 2^{64} different names, do you?

© Dmitri Nesteruk 2018
D. Nesteruk, *Design Patterns in Modern C++*, https://doi.org/10.1007/978-1-4842-3603-1_11

We can actually typedef this to tweak later:

```
1   typedef uint32_t key;
```

With this definition, we can make a user defined as follows:

```
1   struct User
2   {
3     User(const string& first_name, const string& last_name)
4       : first_name{add(first_name)}, last_name{add(last_
        name)} {}
5     ...
6   protected:
7     key first_name, last_name;
8     static bimap<key, string> names;
9     static key seed;
10    static key add(const string& s) { ... }
11  };
```

As you can see, the constructor initializes the members first_name and last_name with the result of calling the add() function. This function inserts the key-value pairs (keys are generated from a seed) into the names structure as necessary. I'm using a boost::bimap (a bidirectional map) here because it's easier to search for duplicates—remember, if the first or last name is already in the bimap, we just return an index to it.

So here is the implementation of add():

```
1   static key add(const string& s)
2   {
3     auto it = names.right.find(s);
4     if (it == names.right.end())
5     {
6       // add it
7       names.insert({++seed, s});
```

```
8      return seed;
9    }
10     return it->second;
11   }
```

This is a fairly standard implementation of the get-or-add mechanic. You might want to consult bimap's documentation for more info on how it works if you haven't met it before.

So now, if we want to actually *expose* the first and last names (the fields are protected and are of type key, not very useful!), we can provide the appropriate getters and setters:

```
1    const string& get_first_name() const
2    {
3      return names.left.find(last_name)->second;
4    }
5
6    const string& get_last_name() const
7    {
8      return names.left.find(last_name)->second;
9    }
```

For example, to define a User's stream output operator, you could simply write

```
1    friend ostream& operator<<(ostream& os, const User& obj)
2    {
3      return os
4        << "first_name: " << obj.get_first_name()
5        << " last_name: " << obj.get_last_name();
6    }
```

And that's it. I am not going to offer statistics on the amount of space saved (this really depends on your sample size), but hopefully it's obvious that, in the case of a large number of repeating user names, the savings are significant—especially if you redice the sizeof(key) further by changing its typedef.

Boost.Flyweight

In the previous example, I have handcrafted a Flyweight, even though I could have reused one avaivalable as a Boost library. The boost::flyweight type does exactly what it says on the tin: constructs a space-saving flyweight.

This makes the implementation of the User class rather trivial:

```
1   struct User2
2   {
3     flyweight<string> first_name, last_name;
4
5     User2(const string& first_name, const string& last_name)
6       : first_name{first_name},
7           last_name{last_name} {}
8   };
```

And you can verify that it *is* in fact a flyweight by running the following code:

```
1   User2 john_doe{ "John", "Doe" };
2   User2 jane_doe{ "Jane", "Doe" };
3   cout << boolalpha <<
4     (&jane_doe.last_name.get() == &john_doe.last_name.get());
      // true
```

String Ranges

If you call `std::string::substring()`, should that return you a brand new constructed string? The jury is out: if you want to manipulate it, then sure, but what if you want changes to the substring to affect the original object? Some programming languages (e.g., Swift, Rust) explicitly return a substring as a *range* which is, again, an implementation of the Flyweight pattern that saves on the amount of memory used, in addition to allowing us to manipulate the underlying object through the range.

The C++ equivalent to a range of a string is a `string_view`, and there are additional variations for arrays—anything to avoid copying data! Let's try to construct our own, very trivial, string range.

Let us suppose that we've got a bunch of text stored in a class, and we want to grab a range of that text and capitalize it, kind of like something a word processor or IDE might do. We *could* just capitalize every individual letter and be done with it, but let's assume we want to keep the underlying plain text in its original state, and only capitalize when we use the stream output operator.

Naïve Approach

A very silly approach would be to define a `boolean` array whose size matches the plain-text string and the value indicates whether we capitalize the character or not. We can implement it like this:

```
1   class FormattedText
2   {
3     string plainText;
4     bool *caps;
5   public:
6     explicit FormattedText(const string& plainText)
7       : plainText{plainText}
```

```
 8      {
 9         caps = new bool[plainText.length()];
10      }
11      ~FormattedText()
12      {
13        delete[] caps;
14      }
15    };
```

We can now make a utility method for capitalizing a particular range:

```
1    void capitalize(int start, int end)
2    {
3      for (int i = start; i <= end; ++i)
4        caps[i] = true;
5    }
```

and then define a stream output operator that makes use of the Boolean mask:

```
1    friend std::ostream& operator<<(std::ostream& os, const
     FormattedText& obj)
2    {
3      string s;
4      for (int i = 0; i < obj.plainText.length(); ++i)
5      {
6        char c = obj.plainText[i];
7        s += (obj.caps[i] ? toupper(c) : c);
8      }
9      return os << s;
10   }
```

Don't get me wrong, this approach works. Here:

```
1   FormattedText ft("This is a brave new world");
2   ft.capitalize(10, 15);
3   cout << ft << endl;
4   // prints "This is a BRAVE new world"
```

But, again, it's very silly to define every single character as having a Boolean flag, when just the start and end markers will do. Let's try to use the Flyweight pattern again.

Flyweight Implementation

Let's implement a BetterFormattedText that makes use of the Flyweight design pattern. We'll begin by defining both the outer class as well as the Flyweight, which I've implemented as a nested class (because why not?):

```
1   class BetterFormattedText
2   {
3   public:
4     struct TextRange
5     {
6       int start, end;
7       bool capitalize;
8       // other options here, e.g. bold, italic, etc.
9
10      bool covers(int position) const
11      {
12        return position >= start && position <= end;
13      }
14    };
15  private:
```

```
16     string plain_text;
17     vector<TextRange> formatting;
18   };
```

As you can see, TextRange just stores the start and end points to which it applies, as well as the actual formatting information—whether we want to capitalize text as well as any other formatting option (bold, italic, etc.). It has just a single member function covers(), which helps us determine whether this piece of formatting needs to be applied to the character at the given position.

BetterFormattedText stores a vector of TextRange flyweights and is able to construct new ones on demand:

```
1   TextRange& get_range(int start, int end)
2   {
3     formatting.emplace_back(TextRange{ start, end });
4     return *formatting.rbegin();
5   }
```

Three things are happening in the preceding example:

1. A new TextRange is construted.

2. It gets moved into the vector.

3. A reference to the last element is returned.

We don't really check duplicate ranges in the preceding implementation—something that would also be in the spirit of Flyweight-based space economy.

We can now implement operator<< for BetterFormattedText:

```
1   friend std::ostream& operator<<(std::ostream& os,
2     const BetterFormattedText& obj)
3   {
4     string s;
```

```
5     for (size_t i = 0; i < obj.plain_text.length(); i++)
6     {
7       auto c = obj.plain_text[i];
8       for (const auto& rng : obj.formatting)
9       {
10        if (rng.covers(i) && rng.capitalize)
11          c = toupper(c);
12        s += c;
13      }
14    }
15    return os << s;
16  }
```

Again, all we do is go through each character and check whether there's any range that covers it. If there is, we apply whatever the range specifies, in our case, capitalization. Note that this set-up allows ranges to freely overlap.

We can now use all that we've constructed to capitalize that same word as before, albeit with a slightly different, more flexible, API:

```
1   BetterFormattedText bft("This is a brave new world");
2   bft.get_range(10, 15).capitalize = true;
3   cout << bft << endl;
4   // prints "This is a BRAVE new world"
```

Summary

The Flyweight pattern is fundamentally a space-saving technique. Its exact incarnations are diverse: sometimes you have the Flyweight being returned as an API token that allows you to perform modifications of whoever has spawned it, whereas at other times the Flyweight is implicit, hiding behind the scenes—as in the case of our User, where the client isn't meant to know about the Flyweight actually being used.

CHAPTER 12

Proxy

When we looked at the Decorator design pattern, we saw the different ways of enhancing the functionality of an object. The Proxy design pattern is similar, but its goal is generally to preserve exactly (or as closely as possible) the API that is being used while offering certain internal ehnancements.

Proxy isn't really a homogeneous API, because the different kinds of proxies people build are quite numerous and serve entirely different purposes. In this chapter we'll take a look at a selection of different proxy objects, and you can find more online.

Smart Pointers

The simplest and most direct illustration of the Proxy pattern is a smart pointer. A smart pointer is a wrapper for a pointer that also keeps a reference count, overrides certain operators, but all in all, it provides you the interface that you would get in an ordinary pointer:

```
1   struct BankAccount
2   {
3     void deposit(int amount) { ... }
4   };
5
6   BankAccount *ba = new BankAccount;
7   ba->deposit(123);
8   auto ba2 = make_shared<BankAccount>();
9   ba2->deposit(123); // same API!
```

© Dmitri Nesteruk 2018
D. Nesteruk, *Design Patterns in Modern C++*, https://doi.org/10.1007/978-1-4842-3603-1_12

So a smart pointer can also be used as a substitute for some locations where an ordinary pointer is expected. For example, if (ba) { ... } is valid whether ba is a pointer or a smart pointer, *ba will, in both cases, get you the underlying object. And so on.

There are, of course, differences. The most obvious one being that you don't have to call delete on a smart pointer. But apart from that, it really tries to be as close to an ordinary pointer as possible.

Property Proxy

The term *property* in other programming languages is used to indicate a field and the set of getter/setter methods for that field. There are no properties in C++[1], but if we want to keep using a field while giving it particular accessor/mutator behaviors, we can build a *property proxy*.

Essentially, a property proxy is a class that can masquerade as the property, so we can define it like this:

```
1    template <typename T> struct Property
2    {
3      T value;
4      Property(const T initial_value)
5      {
6        *this = initial_value;
7      }
8      operator T()
9      {
```

---

[1]If you are OK with non-standard C++, check out __declspec(property), which is impemented in many modern compilers including Clang, Intel, and of course MSVC.

```
10        // perform some getter action
11        return value;
12      }
13      T operator =(T new_value)
14      {
15        // perform some setter action
16        return value = new_value;
17      }
18    };
```

In the preceding implementation, I've added comments to places that you would typically customize (or replace outright), which correspond roughly to the location of getters/setters, if you were to go that route instead.

So, our class Property<T> is essentially a drop-in replacement for T, whatever that happens to be. It works by simply allowing conversion to and from T, letting both use the value field. Now you can use it, say, as a field:

```
1    struct Creature
2    {
3      Property<int> strength{ 10 };
4      Property<int> agility{ 5 };
5    };
```

And the typical operations on a field will work also on a field of a property proxy type:

```
1    Creature creature;
2    creature.agility = 20;
3    auto x = creature.strength;
```

Virtual Proxy

If you try to dereference a `nullptr` or an uninitialized pointer, you're asking for trouble. However, there are situations where you only want the object constructed when it's accessed, and you don't want to allocate it prematurely.

This kind of approach is called *lazy instantiation*. If you know exactly where you're going to need lazy behaviors, you can plan ahead and make special provisions for it. If you don't, well... you can build a proxy that takes an existing object and makes it lazy. We call this a *virtual* proxy because the underlying object might not even exist, so instead of accessing something concrete, we're accessing something virtual.

Imagine a typical Image interface:

```
1    struct Image
2    {
3      virtual void draw() = 0;
4    };
```

An eager (opposite of lazy) implementation of a `Bitmap` would load the image from a file on construction, even if that image isn't actually required for anything. (And yes, the code below is an emulation.)

```
1    struct Bitmap : Image
2    {
3      Bitmap(const string& filename)
4      {
5        cout << "Loading image from " << filename << endl;
6      }
7
8      void draw() override
9      {
10       cout << "Drawing image " << filename << endl;
11     }
12   };
```

The very act of construction of this `Bitmap` will trigger the loading of the image:

```
1    Bitmap img{ "pokemon.png" }; // Loading image from pokemon.png
```

That's not quite what we want. What we want is the kind of bitmap that only loads itself when the `draw()` method is used. Now, I suppose we could jump back into `Bitmap` and make it lazy, but suppose it's set in stone and isn't modifiable (or inheritable, for that matter).

So what we can then build is a virtual proxy that will aggregate the original `Bitmap`, provide an identical interface, and also reuse the original `Bitmap`'s functionality:

```cpp
1    struct LazyBitmap : Image
2    {
3      LazyBitmap(const string& filename)
4        : filename(filename) {}
5      ~LazyBitmap() { delete bmp; }
6      void draw() override
7      {
8        if (!bmp)
9          bmp = new Bitmap(filename);
10       bmp->draw();
11     }
12
13   private:
14     Bitmap *bmp{nullptr};
15     string filename;
16   };
```

Here we are. As you can see, the constructor of this LazyBitmap is a lot less "heavy": all it does is store the name of the file to load the image from, and that's it—the image doesn't actually get loaded.

All of the magic happens in draw(): this is where we check the bmp pointer to see whether the underlying (eager!) bitmap has been constructed. If it hasn't, we construct it, and then call its draw() function to actually draw the image.

Now imagine you have some API that uses an Image type:

```
1   void draw_image(Image& img)
2   {
3     cout << "About to draw the image" << endl;
4     img.draw();
5     cout << "Done drawing the image" << endl;
6   }
```

We can use that API with an instance of LazyBitmap instead of Bitmap (hooray, polymorphism!) to render the image, loading it in a lazy fashion:

```
1   LazyBitmap img{ "pokemon.png" };
2   draw_image(img); // image loaded here
3
4   // About to draw the image
5   // Loading image from pokemon.png
6   // Drawing image pokemon.png
7   // Done drawing the image
```

Communication Proxy

Suppose you call a member function foo() on an object of type Bar. Your typical assumption is that Bar has been allocated on the same machine as the one running your code, and you similarly expect Bar::foo() to execute in the same process.

Now imagine that you make a design decision to move Bar and all its members off to a different machine on the network. But you still want the old code to work! If you want to keep going as before, you'll need a *communication proxy*—a component that proxies the calls "over the wire" and of course collects results, if necessary.

Let's implement a simple ping-pong service to illustrate this. First, we define an interface:

```
1  struct Pingable
2  {
3    virtual wstring ping(const wstring& message) = 0;
4  };
```

If we are building ping-pong in-process, we can implement Pong as follows:

```
1  struct Pong : Pingable
2  {
3    wstring ping(const wstring& message) override
4    {
5      return message + L" pong";
6    }
7  };
```

Basically, you ping a Pong and it appends the word " pong" to the end of the message and returns that message. Notice how I'm not using an ostringstream& here, but instead making a new string on each turn: this API is simple to replicate as a web service.

We can now try out this set-up and see how it works in-process:

```
1  void tryit(Pingable& pp)
2  {
3    wcout << pp.ping(L"ping") << "\n";
4  }
```

155

```
5
6   Pong pp;
7   for (int i = 0; i < 3; ++i)
8   {
9     tryit(pp);
10  }
```

And the end result is that we print "ping pong" three times, just as we wanted.

So now, suppose you decide that the Pingable service relocates to a web server, far, far away. Perhaps you even decide to use some other platform, such as ASP.NET, instead of C++:

```
1   [Route("api/[controller]")]
2   public class PingPongController : Controller
3   {
4     [HttpGet("{msg}")]
5     public string Get(string msg)
6     {
7       return msg + " pong";
8     }
9   } // achievement unlocked: use C# in a C++ book
```

With this set-up, we'll build a communication proxy called RemotePong that will be used in place of Pong. Microsoft's REST SDK comes in handy here.[2]

```
1   struct RemotePong : Pingable
2   {
3     wstring ping(const wstring& message) override
```

---

[2]The Microsoft REST SDK is a C++ library for working with REST services. It is both open-source and cross-platform. You can find it on GitHub: https://github.com/Microsoft/cpprestsdk

```
4     {
5         wstring result;
6         http_client client(U("http://localhost:9149/"));
7         uri_builder builder(U("/api/pingpong/"));
8         builder.append(message);
9         pplx::task<wstring> task = client.request(
10            methods::GET, builder.to_string())
11            .then([=](http_response r)
12            {
13                return r.extract_string();
14            });
15        task.wait();
16        return task.get();
17    }
18  };
```

If you are not used to the REST SDK, the preceding might seem a little bewildering; in addition to the REST support, the SDK uses the Concurrency Runtime, a Microsoft library for, you guessed it, concurrency support.

With this implemented, we can now make a single change:

```
1   RemotePong pp; // was Pong
2   for (int i = 0; i < 3; ++i)
3   {
4       tryit(pp);
5   }
```

And that's it, you get the same output, but the actual implementation can be running on Kestrel in a Docker container somewhere halfway around the world.

Summary

This chapter has presented a number of proxies. Unlike the Decorator pattern, the Proxy doesn't try to expand the functionality of an object by adding new members (unless it can't be helped). All it tries to do is enhance the underlying behavior of existing members.

Plenty of different proxies exist:

- Property proxies are stand-in objects that can replace fields and perform additional operations during assignment and/or access.

- Virtual proxies provide virtual access to the underlying object, and can implement behaviors such as lazy object loading. You may feel like you're working with a real object, but the underlying implementation may not have been created yet, and can, for example, be loaded on demand.

- Communication proxies allow us to change the physical location of the object (e.g., move it to the cloud) but allow us to use pretty much the same API. Of course, in this case the API is just a shim for a remote service such as a REST API.

- Logging proxies allow you to perform logging in addition to calling the underlying functions.

There are lots of other proxies out there, and chances are that the ones you build yourself will not fall into a preexisting category, but will instead perform some action specific to your domain.

PART III

Behavioral Patterns

When most people hear about behavioral patterns, it's mainly in relation to animals and how to get them to do what you want. Well, in a way, all of coding is about programs doing what you want, so behavioral software design patterns cover a very wide range of behaviors that are, nonetheless, quite common in programming.

As an example, consider the domain of software engineering. We have languages that are compiled, which involves lexing, parsing, and a million other things (the Interpreter pattern) and, having constructed an abstract syntax tree (AST) for a program, you might want to analyze the program for possible bugs (the Visitor pattern). All of these are behaviors that are common enough to be expressed as patterns, and this is why we are here today.

Unlike Creational patterns (which are concerned exclusively with the creation of objects) or Structural patterns (which are concerned with composition/aggregation/inheritance of objects), Behavioral design patterns do not follow a central theme. While there are certain similarities between different patterns (e.g., Strategy and Template Method do the same thing in different ways), most patterns present unique approaches to solving a particular problem.

CHAPTER 13

Chain of Responsibility

Consider the typical example of corporate malpractice: insider trading. Say a particular trader has been caught red-handed trading on inside information. Who is to blame for this? If management didn't know, it's the trader. But maybe the trader's peers were in on it, in which case the group manager might be the one responsible. Or perhaps the practice is institutional, in which case it's the CEO who would take the blame.

This is an example of a responsibility chain: you have several different elements of a system who can all process a message one after another. As a concept, it's rather easy to implement, since all that's implied is the use of a list of some kind.

Scenario

Imagine a computer game where each creature has a name and two characteristic values—attack and defense:

```
1   struct Creature
2   {
3     string name;
4     int attack, defense;
5     // constructor and << here
6   };
```

© Dmitri Nesteruk 2018
D. Nesteruk, *Design Patterns in Modern C++*, https://doi.org/10.1007/978-1-4842-3603-1_13

Now, as the creature progresses through the game, it might come up to an item (e.g., a magic sword), or it might end up getting enchanted. In either case, its attack and defense values will be modified by something we'll call a CreatureModifier.

Furthermore, situations where *several* modifiers are applied are not uncommon, so we need to be able to stack modifiers on top of a creature, allowing them to be applied in the order they were attached.

Let's see how we can implement this.

Pointer Chain

In classic Chain of Responsibility (CoR) fashion, we shall implement CreatureModifier as follows:

```cpp
 1   class CreatureModifier
 2   {
 3     CreatureModifier* next{nullptr};
 4   protected:
 5     Creature& creature; // alternative: pointer or shared_ptr
 6   public:
 7     explicit CreatureModifier(Creature& creature)
 8       : creature(creature) {}
 9
10     void add(CreatureModifier* cm)
11     {
12       if (next) next->add(cm);
13       else next = cm;
14     }
15
16     virtual void handle()
17     {
```

```
18      if (next) next->handle(); // critical!
19    }
20  };
```

There are a lot of things happening here, so let's discuss them in turn:

- The class takes and stores a reference to the Creature it
  plans to modify.

- The class doesn't really do much, but it's not abstract:
  all its members have implementations.

- The next member points to an optional
  CreatureModifier following this one. The implication is,
  of course, that the modifier it points to is an inheritor of
  CreatureModifier.

- The function add() adds another creature modifier
  to the modifier chain. This is done recursively: if the
  current modifier is nullptr we set it to that, otherwise
  we traverse the entire chain and put it on the end.

- The function handle() simply handles the next item in
  the chain, if it exists; it has no behavior of its own. The fact
  that it's virtual implies that it's meant to be overridden.

So far, all we have is an implementation of a poor man's append-only
singly linked list. But when we start inheriting from it, things will hopefully
become clearer. For example, here is how you would make a modifier that
would double the creature's attack value:

```
1  class DoubleAttackModifier : public CreatureModifier
2  {
3  public:
4    explicit DoubleAttackModifier(Creature& creature)
5      : CreatureModifier(creature) {}
6
```

```
7      void handle() override
8      {
9        creature.attack *= 2;
10       CreatureModifier::handle();
11     }
12   };
```

All right, finally we're getting somewhere. So this modifier inherits from CreatureModifier, and in its handle() method does two things: doubles the attack value and calls handle() from the base class. That second part is critical: the only way in which a *chain* of modifiers can be applied is if every inheritor doesn't forget to call the base at the end of its own handle() implementation.

Here is another, more complicated modifier. This modifier increases the defense of creatures with attack of 2 or less by 1:

```
1    class IncreaseDefenseModifier : public CreatureModifier
2    {
3    public:
4      explicit IncreaseDefenseModifier(Creature& creature)
5        : CreatureModifier(creature) {}
6
7      void handle() override
8      {
9        if (creature.attack <= 2)
10         creature.defense += 1;
11       CreatureModifier::handle();
12     }
13   };
```

Again we call the base class at the end. Putting it all together, we can now make a creature and apply a combination of modifiers to it:

```
1    Creature goblin{ "Goblin", 1, 1 };
2    CreatureModifier root{ goblin };
3    DoubleAttackModifier r1{ goblin };
4    DoubleAttackModifier r1_2{ goblin };
5    IncreaseDefenseModifier r2{ goblin };
6
7    root.add(&r1);
8    root.add(&r1_2);
9    root.add(&r2);
10
11   root.handle();
12
13   cout << goblin << endl;
14   // name: Goblin attack: 4 defense: 1
```

As you can see, the goblin is a 4/1 because its attack got doubled twice and the defense modifier, while added, did not affect its defense score.

Here's another curious point. Suppose you decide to cast a spell on a creature such that no bonus can be applied to it. Is it easy to do? Quite easy, actually, because all you have to do is avoid calling the base handle(): this avoids executing the entire chain:

```
1    class NoBonusesModifier : public CreatureModifier
2    {
3    public:
4      explicit NoBonusesModifier(Creature& creature)
5        : CreatureModifier(creature) {}
6
7      void handle() override
8      {
```

```
9        // nothing here!
10    }
11  };
```

That's it! Now, if you slot the NoBonusesModifier at the *beginning* of the chain, no further elements will be applied.

Broker Chain

The example with the pointer chain is very artificial. In the real world, you'd want creatures to be able to take on and lose bonuses arbitrarily, something which an append-only linked list doesn't support. Furthermore, you don't want to modify the underlying creature stats permanently (as we did)—instead, you want to keep modifications temporary.

One way to implement CoR is through a centralized component. This component can keep a list of *all* modifiers available in the game, and can facilitate queries for a particular creature's attack or defense by ensuring that all relevant bonuses are applied.

The component that we are going to build is called an *event broker*. Since it's connected to every participating component, it represents the Mediator design pattern and, further, since it responds to queries through events, it leverages the Observer design pattern.

Let's build one. First of all, we'll define a structure called Game that will represent, well, a game that's being played:

```
1   struct Game // mediator
2   {
3     signal<void(Query&)> queries;
4   };
```

We are using the Boost.Signals2 library for keeping a *signal* called queries. Essentially, what this lets us do is fire this signal and have it handled by every slot (listening component). But what do events have to do with querying a creature's attack or defense?

Well, imagine that you want to query a creature's statistic. You could certainly try to read a field, but remember: we need to apply all the modifiers before the final value is known. So instead we'll encapsulate a query in a separate object (this is the Command pattern[1]) defined as follows:

```
1   struct Query
2   {
3       string creature_name;
4       enum Argument { attack, defense } argument;
5       int result;
6   };
```

All we've done in the aforementioned class is encapsulated the concept of querying a particular value from a creature. All we need to provide is the name of the creature and which statistic we're interested in. It is precisely this value (well, a reference to it) that will be constructed and used by Game::queries to apply the modifiers and return the final value.

Now, let's move on to the definition of Creature. It's very similar to what we had before. The only difference in terms of fields is a reference to a Game:

```
1   class Creature
2   {
3       Game& game;
4       int attack, defense;
5   public:
6       string name;
```

---

[1]Actually, there's a bit of confusion here. The concept of Command Query Separation (CQS) suggests the separation of operations into commands (which mutate state and yield no value) and queries (which do not mutate anything but yield a value). The GoF does not have a concept of a Query, so we let any encapsulated instruction to a component be called a Command.

```
7     Creature(Game& game, ...) : game{game}, ... { ... }
8     // other members here
9   };
```

Now, notice how attack and defense are private. This means that, to get at the *final* (post-modifier) attack value, you would need to call a separate getter function, for example:

```
1   int Creature::get_attack() const
2   {
3     Query q{ name, Query::Argument::attack, attack };
4     game.queries(q);
5     return q.result;
6   }
```

This is where the magic happens! Instead of just returning a value or statically applying some pointer-based chain, what we do is create a Query with the right arguments and then send the query off to be handled by whoever is subscribed to Game::queries. Every single subscribed component gets a chance to modify the baseline attack value.

So let's now implement the modifiers. Once again, we'll make a base class, but this time round it won't have a handle() method:

```
1   class CreatureModifier
2   {
3     Game& game;
4     Creature& creature;
5   public:
6     CreatureModifier(Game& game, Creature& creature)
7       : game(game), creature(creature) {}
8   };
```

So the modifier base class isn't particularly interesting. In fact, you could get away with not using it at all, since all it does is ensure that the constructor is called with the right arguments. But since we've gone with this approach, let's now inherit CreatureModifier and see how one would perform actual modifications:

```
1   class DoubleAttackModifier : public CreatureModifier
2   {
3     connection conn;
4   public:
5     DoubleAttackModifier(Game& game, Creature& creature)
6       : CreatureModifier(game, creature)
7     {
8       conn = game.queries.connect([&](Query& q)
9       {
10        if (q.creature_name == creature.name &&
11            q.argument == Query::Argument::attack)
12          q.result *= 2;
13      });
14    }
15
16    ~DoubleAttackModifier() { conn.disconnect(); }
17  };
```

As you can see, all the fun happens in the constructor and destructor; no additional methods are required. In the constructor, we use the Game reference to grab hold of the Game::queries signal and connect to it, specifying a lambda that doubles the attack. Naturally, the lambda must make a couple of checks: we need to make sure that we are augmenting the right creature (we compare by name) and that the statistic we're after is, in fact, attack. Both pieces of information are kept inside the Query reference, as is the initial result value that we modify.

We also take care to store the signal connection so that we break it when the object is destroyed. That way, we can apply the modifier temporarily and let it fizzle out when, for example, the modifier goes out of scope.

Putting it all together, we get the following:

```
1   Game game;
2   Creature goblin{ game, "Strong Goblin", 2, 2 };
3   cout << goblin << endl;
4   // name: Strong Goblin attack: 2 defense: 2
5   {
6     DoubleAttackModifier dam{ game, goblin };
7     cout << goblin << endl;
8     // name: Strong Goblin attack: 4 defense: 2
9   }
10  cout << goblin << endl;
11  // name: Strong Goblin attack: 2 defense: 2
12  }
```

What's happening here? Well, prior to being modified, the goblin is a 2/2. Then, we manufacture a scope, within which the goblin is affected by a DoubleAttackModifier, so inside the scope it is a 4/2 creature. As soon as we exit the scope, the modifier's destructor triggers and it disconnects itself from the broker and thus no longer affects the values when they are queried. Consequently, the goblin itself reverts to being a 2/2 creature once again.

Summary

Chain of Responsibility is a very simple design pattern that lets components process a command (or a query) in turn. The simplest implementation of CoR is one where you simply make a pointer chain and, in theory, you could replace it with just an ordinary vector or, perhaps, a list if you wanted fast removal as well.

A more sophisticated Broker Chain implementation that also leverages the Mediator and Observer patterns allows us to process queries on an event (signal), letting each subscriber perform modifications of the originally passed object (it's a single reference that goes through the entire chain) before the final values are returned to the client.

CHAPTER 14

Command

Think about a trivial variable assignment, such as `meaning_of_life = 42`. The variable got assigned, but there's no record anywhere that the assignment took place. Nobody can give us the previous value. We cannot take the *fact* of assignment and serialize it somewhere. This is problematic, because without a record of the change, we are unable to roll back to previous values, perform audits, or do history-based debugging.[1]

The Command design pattern proposes that, instead of working with objects directly by manipulating them through their APIs, we send them *commands*: instructions on how to do something. A command is nothing more than a data class with its members describing what to do and how to do it. Let's take a look at a typical scenario.

Scenario

Let's try to model a typical bank account that has a balance and an overdraft limit. We'll implement `deposit()` and `withdraw()` functions on it:

```
1    struct BankAccount
2    {
3      int balance = 0;
4      int overdraft_limit = -500;
5
```

---

[1] We do have dedicated historical debugging tools such as Visual Studio's IntelliTrace or UndoDB.

© Dmitri Nesteruk 2018
D. Nesteruk, *Design Patterns in Modern C++*, https://doi.org/10.1007/978-1-4842-3603-1_14

```
6      void deposit(int amount)
7      {
8        balance += amount;
9        cout << "deposited " << amount << ", balance is now "
<<
10         balance << "\n";
11     }
12
13     void withdraw(int amount)
14     {
15       if (balance - amount >= overdraft_limit)
16       {
17         balance -= amount;
18         cout << "withdrew " << amount << ", balance is now " <<
19           balance << "\n";
20       }
21     }
22   };
```

Now we can call the member functions directly, of course, but let us suppose that, for audit purposes, we need to make a record of every deposit and withdrawal made and we cannot do it right inside BankAccount because—guess what—we've already designed, implemented, and tested that class.

Implementing the Command Pattern

We'll begin by defining an interface for a command:

```
1    struct Command
2    {
3      virtual void call() const = 0;
4    };
```

Having made the interface, we can now use it to define a
BankAccountCommand that will encapsulate information about what to do
with a bank account:

```
1    struct BankAccountCommand : Command
2    {
3      BankAccount& account;
4      enum Action { deposit, withdraw } action;
5      int amount;
6
7      BankAccountCommand(BankAccount& account, const Action
8      action, const int amount)
9        : account(account), action(action), amount(amount) {}
```

The information contained in the command includes the following:

- The account to operate upon

- The action to take; both the set of options and the
  variable to store those options is defined in a single
  declaration

- The amount to deposit or withdraw

Once the client provides this information, we can take it and use it to perform the deposit or withdrawal:

```
1   void call() const override
2   {
3     switch (action)
4     {
5     case deposit:
6       account.deposit(amount);
7       break;
8     case withdraw:
9       account.withdraw(amount);
10      break;
11    }
12  }
```

With this approach, we can create the command and then perform modifications of the account right on the command:

```
1   BankAccount ba;
2   Command cmd{ba, BankAccountCommand::deposit, 100};
3   cmd.call();
```

This will deposit 100 dollars into our account. Easy! And if you're worried that we're still exposing the original deposit() and withdraw() member functions to the client, you can make them private and simply designate BankAccountCommand as a friend class.

Undo Operations

Since a command encapsulates all information about some modification to a BankAccount, it can equally roll back this modification and return its target object to its prior state.

To begin with, we need to decide whether to stick undo-related operations into our Command interface. I will do it here for purposes of brevity, but in general, this is a design decision that needs to respect the Interface Segregation Principle that we discussed at the beginning of the book (Chapter 1). For example, if you envisage some commands being final and not subject to undo mechanics, it might make sense to split Command into, say, Callable and Undoable.

Anyways, here's the updated Command; note I have deliberately removed const from the functions:

```
1    struct Command
2    {
3      virtual void call() = 0;
4      virtual void undo() = 0;
5    };
```

And here is a naïve implementation of BankAccountCommand::undo(), motivated by the (incorrect) assumption that account deposit and withdrawal are symmetric operations:

```
1    void undo() override
2    {
3      switch (action)
4      {
5      case withdraw:
6        account.deposit(amount);
7        break;
8      case deposit:
9        account.withdraw(amount);
10       break;
11     }
12   }
```

Why is this implementation broken? Because if you tried to withdraw an amount equal to the GDP of a developed nation, you would not be successful, but when rolling back the transaction, we don't have a way of telling that it failed!

To get this information, we modify withdraw() to return a success flag:

```cpp
1   bool withdraw(int amount)
2   {
3     if (balance - amount >= overdraft_limit)
4     {
5       balance -= amount;
6       cout << "withdrew " << amount << ", balance now " <<
7         balance << "\n";
8       return true;
9     }
10    return false;
11  }
```

That's much better! We can now modify the entire BankAccountCommand to do two things:

- Store internally a success flag when a withdrawal is made.

- Use this flag when undo() is called.

Here we go:

```cpp
1   struct BankAccountCommand : Command
2   {
3     ...
4     bool withdrawal_succeeded;
5
6     BankAccountCommand(BankAccount& account, const Action action,
7       const int amount)
```

```
 8        : ..., withdrawal_succeeded{false} {}
 9
10     void call() override
11     {
12       switch (action)
13       {
14         ...
15       case withdraw:
16         withdrawal_succeeded = account.withdraw(amount);
17         break;
18       }
19     }
```

Do you now see why I removed const from the members of Command? Now that we are assigning a member variable withdrawal_succeeded, we can no longer claim that call() is const. I suppose I could have kept it on undo(), but there's very little benefit in that.

Okay, so now we have the flag, we can improve our implementation of undo():

```
 1     void undo() override
 2     {
 3       switch (action)
 4       {
 5       case withdraw:
 6         if (withdrawal_succeeded)
 7           account.deposit(amount);
 8         break;
 9         ...
10       }
11     }
```

Tada! We can finally undo withdraw commands in a consistent fashion.

The goal of this exercise was, of course, to illustrate that, in addition to storing information about the action to perform, a Command can also store some intermediate information that is, once again, useful for things like audits: if you detect a series of 100 failed withdrawal attempts, you can investigate a potential hack.

Composite Command

A transfer of money from account A to account B can be simulated with two commands:

1. Withdraw $X from A

2. Deposit $X to B

It would be nice if, instead of creating and calling these two commands, we could just create and call a single command that encapsulates both of the commands. This is the essence of the Composite design pattern that we discussed in Chapter 8.

Let's define a skeleton composite command. I'm going to inherit from vector <BankAccountCommand>—this can be problematic since std::vector doesn't have a virtual destructor, but it's not a problem in our case. So here is a very simple definition:

```
1  struct CompositeBankAccountCommand : vector
   <BankAccountCommand>, Command
2  {
3    CompositeBankAccountCommand(const initializer_list
     <value_type>& items)
4      : vector<BankAccountCommand>(items) {}
5
6  void call() override
```

```
7     {
8       for (auto& cmd : *this)
9         cmd.call();
10    }
11
12    void undo() override
13    {
14      for (auto it = rbegin(); it != rend(); ++it)
15        it->undo();
16    }
17  };
```

As you can see, the CompositeBankAccountCommand is both a vector as well as a Command, which fits the definition of the Composite design pattern. I've added a constructor that takes an initializer list (very useful!) and implemented both undo() and redo() operations. Note that the undo() process goes through commands in reverse order; hopefully I don't have to explain *why* you'd want this as default behavior.

So now, how about a composite command specifically for transferring money? I would define it as follows:

```
1   struct MoneyTransferCommand : CompositeBankAccountCommand
2   {
3     MoneyTransferCommand(BankAccount& from,
4       BankAccount& to, int amount) :
5       CompositeBankAccountCommand
6       {
7         BankAccountCommand{from, BankAccountCommand::
         withdraw, amount},
8         BankAccountCommand{to, BankAccountCommand::deposit,
         amount}
9       } {}
10  };
```

As you can see, all we're doing is reusing the base class constructor to intialize the object with the two commands, and then reuse the base class' call()/undo() implementations.

But wait, that's not right, is it? The base class implementations don't quite cut it because they don't incorporate the idea of failure. If I fail to withdraw money from A, I shouldn't deposit that money to B: the entire chain should cancel itself.

To support this idea, more drastic changes are required. We need to

- Add a success flag to Command.

- Record the success or failure of *every* operation.

- Ensure that the command can only be undone if it originally succeeded.

- Introduce a new in-between class called DependentCompositeCommand that is very careful about actually rolling back the commands.

When calling each command, we only do so if the previous one succeeded; otherwise we simply set the success flag to false.

```
1    void call() override
2    {
3      bool ok = true;
4      for (auto& cmd : *this)
5      {
6        if (ok)
7        {
8          cmd.call();
9          ok = cmd.succeeded;
10       }
11       else
12       {
```

```
13            cmd.succeeded = false;
14        }
15    }
16  }
```

There is no need to override the undo() because each of our commands checks its own success flag and undoes the operation only if it's set to true.

One can imagine an even stronger form of the preceding where a composite command only succeeds if *all* of its parts succeed (think about a transfer where the withdrawal succeeds but the deposit fails—would you want it to go through?) —this is a bit harder to implement, and I again leave it as an exercise for the reader.

The entire purpose of this section is to illustrate how a simple Command-based approach can get quite complicated when real-world business requirements are taken into account. Whether or not you actually *need* this complexity... well, that is up to you.

Command Query Separation

The notion of Command Query Separation (CQS) is the idea that operations in a system fall broadly into the following two categories:

- Commands, which are instructions for the system to perform some operation that involves mutation of state but yields no value

- Queries, which are requests for information that yield values but do not mutate state

Any object that presently exposes its state directly for reading and writing can hide its state (make it private) and then, instead of providing getter and setter pairs, can offer a singular interface. Here's what I mean: suppose we have a Creature with two properties called strength and agility. We can define the creature thus:

```
1    class Creature
2    {
3      int strength, agility;
4    public:
5      Creature(int strength, int agility)
6        : strength{strength}, agility{agility} {}
7
8      void process_command(const CreatureCommand& cc);
9      int process_query(const CreatureQuery& q) const;
10   };
```

As you can see, there are no getters and setters, but we do have two (just two!) API members called process_command() and process_query() that are meant to be used for *all* interactions with Creature objects. Both of these are dedicated classes which, together with the CreatureAbility enumeration, are defined as follows:

```
1    enum class CreatureAbility { strength, agility };
2
3    struct CreatureCommand
4    {
5      enum Action { set, increaseBy, decreaseBy } action;
6      CreatureAbility ability;
7      int amount;
8    };
9
10   struct CreatureQuery
```

```
11   {
12     CreatureAbility ability;
13   };
```

As you can see, the command describes what member you want to change and how you want to change it, and by how much. The query object only specifies what to query, and we assume that the result of the query is returned from the function, rather than set in the query object itself (if other objects affect this one, as we have seen already, that's how you would do it instead).

So here is the process_command() definition:

```
1   void Creature::process_command(const CreatureCommand &cc)
2   {
3     int* ability;
4     switch (cc.ability)
5     {
6       case CreatureAbility::strength:
7         ability = &strength;
8         break;
9       case CreatureAbility::agility:
10         ability = &agility;
11         break;
12     }
13     switch (cc.action)
14     {
15       case CreatureCommand::set:
16         *ability = cc.amount;
17         break;
18       case CreatureCommand::increaseBy:
19         *ability += cc.amount;
20         break;
```

```
21          case CreatureCommand::decreaseBy:
22            *ability -= cc.amount;
23            break;
24      }
25    }
```

And here is the much simpler process_query() definition:

```
1    int Creature::process_query(const CreatureQuery &q) const
2    {
3      switch (q.ability)
4      {
5        case CreatureAbility::strength: return strength;
6        case CreatureAbility::agility: return agility;
7      }
8      return 0;
9    }
```

If you want logging or persistence of these command and queries, you now have just two locations where this needs to be done. The only real issue with all of this is how difficult the API is to work with for someone who just wants to manipulate the object in a familiar manner.

Luckily for us, we can always manufacture getter/setter pairs if we want to; these would just call the process_ methods with appropriate arguments:

```
1    void Creature::set_strength(int value)
2    {
3      process_command(CreatureCommand{
4        CreatureCommand::set, CreatureAbility::strength, value
5      });
6    }
7
```

```
 8    int Creature::get_strength() const
 9    {
10      return process_query(CreatureQuery{CreatureAbility::
        strength});
11    }
```

The preceding is, admittedly, a very simplistic illustration of what actually happens inside systems that do CQS, but it hopefully gives an idea of how one can split *all* object interfaces into Command and Query parts.

Summary

The Command design pattern is simple: what it basically suggests is that objects can communicate with one another using special objects that encapsulate instructions, rather than specifying those same instructions as arguments to a method.

Sometimes, you don't want such an object to mutate the target or cause it to do something specific; instead you want to use such an object to inquire a value from the target, in which case we typically call such an object a Query. While, in most cases, a query is an immutable object that relies on the return type of the method, there *are* situations (see, e.g., the Chain of Responsibility Broker Chain example; Chapter 13) when you want the result that's being returned to be modified by other components. But the components themselves are still not modified, only the result is.

Commands are used a lot in UI systems to encapsulate typical actions (e.g., Copy or Paste) and then allow a single command to be invoked by several different means. For example, you can Copy by using the top-level application menu, a button on the toolbar, or a keyboard shortcut. Finally, these actions can be combined into macros—sequences of actions that can be recorded and then replayed at will.

CHAPTER 15

Interpreter

The goal of the Interpreter design pattern is, you guessed it, to interpret input, particularly *textual* input, although to be fair it really doesn't matter. The notion of an Interpreter is greatly linked to Compiler Theory and similar courses taught at universities. Since we don't have nearly enough space here to delve into the complexities of different types of parsers and whatnot, the purpose of this chapter is to simply show some examples of the kinds of things you might want to interpret.

Here are a few fairly obvious ones:

- Numeric literals such as 42 or 1.234e12 need to be interpreted to be stored efficiently in binary. In C++, these operations are covered both via C APIs such as atof() as well as more sophisticated libraries such as Boost.LexicalCast.

- Regular expressions help us find patterns in text, but what you need to realize is that regular expressions are essentially a separate, embedded domain-specific language (DSL). And naturally, before using them, they must be interpreted correctly.

- Any structured data, be it CSV, XML, JSON, or something more complicated, requires interpretation before it can be used.

© Dmitri Nesteruk 2018
D. Nesteruk, *Design Patterns in Modern C++*, https://doi.org/10.1007/978-1-4842-3603-1_15

- At the pinnacle of the application of Interpreter, we have fully fledged programming languages. After all, a compiler or interpreter for a language like C or Python must actually understand the language before making something executable.

Given the proliferation and diversity of challenges related to interpretation, we shall simply look at some examples. These serve to illustrate how one can build an Interpreter: either by making something from scratch or by leveraging a library that helps do these things at an industrial scale.

Numeric Expression Evaluator

Let's imagine that we decide to parse *very* simple mathematical expressions such as 3+(5–4), that is, we'll restrict ourselves to addition, subtraction, and brackets. We want a program that can read such an expression and, of course, calculate the expression's final value.

We are going to build the calculator *by hand*, without resorting to any parsing framework. This should hopefully highlight *some* of the complexity involved in parsing textual input.

Lexing

The first step to interpreting an expression is called *lexing*, and it involves turning a sequence of characters into a sequence of *tokens*. A token is typically a primitive syntactic element, and we should end up with a flat sequence of these. In our case, a token can be

- An integer

- An operator (plus or minus)

- An opening or closing parenthesis

Thus, we can define the following structure:

```
1   struct Token
2   {
3     enum Type { integer, plus, minus, lparen, rparen } type;
4     string text;
5
6     explicit Token(Type type, const string& text)
7       : type{type}, text{text} {}
8
9     friend ostream& operator<<(ostream& os, const
      Token& obj)
10    {
11      return os << "`" << obj.text << "`";
12    }
13  };
```

You'll note that Token is not an enum because, apart from the type, we also want to store the text that this token relates to, since it is not always predefined.

So now, given an std::string containing an expression, we can define a lexing process that will turn a text into a vector<Token>:

```
1   vector<Token> lex(const string& input)
2   {
3     vector<Token> result;
4
5     for (int i = 0; i < input.size(); ++i)
6     {
7       switch (input[i])
8       {
9       case '+':
10        result.push_back(Token{ Token::plus, "+" });
11        break;
```

```
12          case '-':
13              result.push_back(Token{ Token::minus, "-" });
14              break;
15          case '(':
16              result.push_back(Token{ Token::lparen, "(" });
17              break;
18          case ')':
19              result.push_back(Token{ Token::rparen, ")" });
20              break;
21          default:
22              // number ???
23          }
24      }
25  }
```

Parsing predefined tokens is easy. In fact, we could have added them as a map<BinaryOperation, char> to simplify things. But parsing a number is not so easy. If we hit a 1, we should wait and see what the next character is. For this we define a separate routine:

```
1   ostringstream buffer;
2   buffer << input[i];
3   for (int j = i + 1; j < input.size(); ++j)
4   {
5     if (isdigit(input[j]))
6     {
7       buffer << input[j];
8       ++i;
9     }
10    else
11    {
12      result.push_back(Token{ Token::integer, buffer.str() });
```

```
13        break;
14    }
15  }
```

Essentially, while we keep reading (pumping) digits, we add them to the buffer. When we're done, we make a Token out of the entire buffer and add it to the resulting vector.

Parsing

The process of *parsing* turns a sequence of tokens into meaningful, typically object-oriented, structures. At the top, it's often useful to have an abstract parent type that all elements of the tree implement:

```
1   struct Element
2   {
3     virtual int eval() const = 0;
4   };
```

The type's eval() function evaluates this element's numeric value. Next, we can create an element for storing integral values (such as 1, 5, or 42):

```
1   struct Integer : Element
2   {
3     int value;
4
5     explicit Integer(const int value)
6       : value(value) {}
7
8     int eval() const override { return value; }
9   };
```

If we don't have an `Integer`, we must have an operation such as addition or subtraction. In our case, all operations are *binary*, meaning they have two parts. For example, 2+3 in our model can be represented in pseudocode as `BinaryOperation{Literal{2}, Literal{3}, addition}`:

```
1   struct BinaryOperation : Element
2   {
3     enum Type { addition, subtraction } type;
4     shared_ptr<Element> lhs, rhs;
5
6     int eval() const override
7     {
8       if (type == addition)
9         return lhs->eval() + rhs->eval();
10      return lhs->eval() - rhs->eval();
11    }
12  };
```

Note that, in the preceding, I'm using an enum instead of an enum `class` so that I can write `BinaryOperation::addition` later on.

But anyways, on to the parsing process. All we need to do is turn a sequence of Tokens into a binary tree of Expressions. From the outset, it can look as follows:

```
1   shared_ptr<Element> parse(const vector<Token>& tokens)
2   {
3     auto result = make_unique<BinaryOperation>();
4     bool have_lhs = false; // this will need some explaining :)
5     for (size_t i = 0; i < tokens.size(); i++)
6     {
7       auto token = tokens[i];
8       switch(token.type)
```

```
 9       {
10           // process each of the tokens in turn
11       }
12     }
13     return result;
14   }
```

The only thing we need to discuss from the preceding code is the have_lhs variable. Remember, what you are trying to get is a tree, and at the *root* of that tree we expect a BinaryExpression which, by definition, has left and right sides. But when we are on a number, how do we know if it's the left or right side of an expression? That's right, we don't, which is why we track this.

Now let's go through these case by case. First, integers—these map directly to our Integer construct, so all we have to do is turn text into a number. (Incidentally, we could have also done this at the lexing stage if we wanted to.)

```
 1   case Token::integer:
 2   {
 3     int value = boost::lexical_cast<int>(token.text);
 4     auto integer = make_shared<Integer>(value);
 5     if (!have_lhs) {
 6       result->lhs = integer;
 7       have_lhs = true;
 8     }
 9     else result->rhs = integer;
10   }
```

The plus and minus tokens simply determine the type of the operation we're currently processing, so they're easy:

```
1    case Token::plus:
2      result->type = BinaryOperation::addition;
3      break;
4    case Token::minus:
5      result->type = BinaryOperation::subtraction;
6      break;
```

And then there's the left parenthesis. Yep, just the left, we don't detect the right one explicitly on this level. Basically, the idea here is simple: find the closing right parenthesis (I'm ignoring nested brackets for now), rip out the entire subexpression, parse() it recursively, and set as the left or right-hand side of the expression we're currently working with:

```
1    case Token::lparen:
2    {
3      int j = i;
4      for (; j < tokens.size(); ++j)
5        if (tokens[j].type == Token::rparen)
6          break; // found it!
7
8      vector<Token> subexpression(&tokens[i + 1], &tokens[j]);
9      auto element = parse(subexpression); // recursive call
10     if (!have_lhs)
11     {
12       result->lhs = element;
13       have_lhs = true;
14     }
15     else result->rhs = element;
16     i = j; // advance
17   }
```

In a real-world scenario, you'd want a lot more safety features in here: not just handling nested parentheses (which I think is a must), but handling incorrect expressions where the closing parenthesis is missing. If it is indeed missing, how would you handle it? Throw an exception? Try to parse whatever's left and assume the closing is at the very end? Something else? All of these issues are left as an exercise for the reader.

From experience with C++ itself, we know that making meaningful error messages for parsing errors is *very* hard. In fact, you will find a phenomenon called *skipping* where, in doubt, the lexer or parser will attempt to skip incorrect code until it meets something meaningful: precisely this approach is adopted by static analysis tools that are expected to work correctly on incomplete code as the user is typing it.

Using Lexer and Parser

With both `lex()` and `parse()` implemented, we can finally parse the expression and calculate its value:

```
1    string input{ "(13-4)-(12+1)" };
2    auto tokens = lex(input);
3    auto parsed = parse(tokens);
4    cout << input << " = " << parsed->eval() << endl;
5    // prints "(13-4)-(12+1) = -4"
```

Parsing with Boost.Spirit

In the real world, hardly anyone hand-rolls parsers for something complicated. Sure, if you are parsing a "trivial" data storage format such as XML or JSON, hand-rolling the parser is easy. But if you are implementing your own DSL or programming language, this is not an option.

Boost.Spirit is a library that helps the creation of parsers by providing succint (though not particularly intuitive) APIs for the construction of parsers. The library does not attempt to explicitly separate the lexing and parsing stages (unless you really want to), allowing you to define how textual constructs get mapped onto objects of types you define.

Let me show you some examples of using Boost.Spirit with the Tlön programming language.[1]

Abstract Syntax Tree

To start with, you need your AST (Abstract Syntax Tree). In this respect, I simply make a base class that supports the Visitor design pattern, since traversal of these structures is very important:

```
1   struct ast_element
2   {
3     virtual ~ast_element() = default;
4     virtual void accept(ast_element_visitor& visitor) = 0;
5   };
```

This interface is then used to define different code constructs in my language, for example:

```
1   struct property : ast_element
2   {
3     vector<wstring> names;
4     type_specification type;
5     bool is_constant{ false };
6     wstring default_value;
7
```

---

[1]Tlön is a toy language that I built to demo the idea of "if you don't like existing languages, build a new one." It uses Boost.Spirit and cross-compiles (transpiles) into C++. It is open-source and can be found at https://github.com/nesteruk/tlon

```
8     void accept(ast_element_visitor& visitor) override
9     {
10       visitor.visit(*this);
11    }
12  };
```

The preceding definition of a property has four different parts, each stored in a publicly accessible field. Note that it uses a type_specification, which is itself another ast_element.

Every single class of an AST needs to be adapted for Boost.Fusion—another Boost library that supports a fusion (hence the name) of compile time (metaprogramming) and runtime algorithms. The adaptation code is simple enough:

```
1   BOOST_FUSION_ADAPT_STRUCT(
2     tlön::property,
3     (std::vector<std::wstring>, names),
4     (tlön::type_specification, type),
5     (bool, is_constant),
6     (std::wstring, default_value)
7   )
```

Spirit has no trouble parsing into common data types such as a std::vector or std::optional. It does have a bit more problems with polymorphism: rather than having your AST types inherit from one another, Spirit prefers that you use a variant, that is:

```
1   typedef variant<function_body, property, function_
    signature> class_member;
```

Parser

Boost.Spirit lets us define the parser as a set of rules. The syntax that is used is very similar to regular expressions or BNF (Bachus-Naur Form) notation, except the operators are placed *before* the symbol, not after. Here is an example rule:

```
1    class_declaration_rule %=
2       lit(L"class ") >> +(alnum) % '.'
3       >> -(lit(L"(") >> -parameter_declaration_rule % ',' >>
         lit(")"))
4       >> "{"
5       >> *(function_body_rule | property_rule | function_
         signature_rule)
6       >> "}";
```

The preceding expects a class declaration to start with the word class. It then expects one or more words (each word is one or more alphanumeric characters, thus +(alnum)), separated with periods '.'—this is what the % operator is used for. The result, as you may have guessed, would map onto a vector. Subsequently, after the curly braces, we expect zero or more definitions of functions, properties, or function signatures—the fields these would be mapped to correspond to our prior definition using a variant.

Naturally, some element is the "root" of the entire hierarchy of AST elements. In our case, this root is called a file (surprise!), and here is a function that both parses the file and pretty-prints it:

```
1    template<typename TLanguagePrinter, typename Iterator>
2    wstring parse(Iterator first, Iterator last)
3    {
4      using spirit::qi::phrase_parse;
5
6      file f;
7      file_parser<wstring::const_iterator> fp{};
```

```
8      auto b = phrase_parse(first, last, fp, space, f);
9      if (b)
10     {
11        return TLanguagePrinter{}.pretty_print(f);
12     }
13     return wstring(L"FAIL");
14   }
```

The type TLanguagePrinter in the preceding is essentially a visitor that knows how to render our AST in a different language, such as C++.

Printer

Having parsed the language, we might want to compile it or, in my case, transpile it into some other language. This is rather easy considering that we have previously implemented an accept() method into the entire AST hierarchy.

The only challenge is what to do with the variant types, because those need special visitors. In the case of std::variant, what you are after is std::visit(), but since we are using a boost::variant, the function to call for is boost::accept_visitor(). This function requires that you give it an instance of a class inheriting from static_visitor, with function call overloads for every possible type. Here's an example:

```
1    struct default_value_visitor : static_visitor<>
2    {
3      cpp_printer& printer;
4
5      explicit default_value_visitor(cpp_printer& printer)
6        : printer{printer}
7      {
8      }
9
```

```
10      void operator()(const basic_type& bt) const
11      {
12        // for a scalar value, we just dump its default
13        printer.buffer << printer.default_value_for(bt.name);
14      }
15
16      void operator()(const tuple_signature& ts) const
17      {
18        for (auto& e : ts.elements)
19        {
20          this->operator()(e.type);
21          printer.buffer << ", ";
22        }
23        printer.backtrack(2);
24      }
25    };
```

You would then call accept_visitor(foo, default_value_
visitor{...}) and the correct overload will be called depending on the
type of object actually stored in the variant.

Summary

First of all, it needs to be said that, comparatively speaking, the Interpreter
design pattern is somewhat uncommon—the challenge of building parsers
is nowadays considered inessential, which is why I see it being removed
from Computer Science courses in many UK universities (my own
included). Also, unless you plan to work in language design or, say, making
tools for static code analysis, you are unlikely to find the skills in building
parsers in high demand.

That said, the challenge of interpretation is a whole separate field of Computer Science that a single chapter of a Design Patterns book cannot reasonably do justice to. If you are interested in the subject, I recommend you check out frameworks such as Lex/Yacc, ANTLR, and many others that are specifically geared for lexer/parser construction. I can also recommend writing static analysis plug-ins for popular IDEs—this is a great way to get a feel for how real ASTs look, are traversed, and even modified.

CHAPTER 16

Iterator

Any time you start working with complicated data structures, you encounter the problem of *traversal*. This can be handled in different ways, but the most common way of traversing, say, a vector is using something called an *iterator*.

An iterator is, quite simply, an object that can point to an element of a collection and also knows how to move to the next element in the collection. As such, it is only required to implement the ++ operator and the != operator (so you can compare two iterators and check if they point to the same thing). That's it.

The C++ Standard Library makes heavy use of iterators, so we shall discuss the way they are used there, and then we'll take a look at how to make our own iterators and what the limitations of iterators are.

Iterators in the Standard Library

Imagine you have a list of names such as:

```
1   vector<string> names{ "john", "jane", "jill", "jack" };
```

If you want to get the first name in the names collection, you call a function called begin(). This function doesn't give you the first name by value or by reference; instead, it gives you an iterator:

```
1   vector<string>::iterator it = names.begin();
    // begin(names)
```

D. Nesteruk, *Design Patterns in Modern C++*, https://doi.org/10.1007/978-1-4842-3603-1_16
205

The function begin() exists as both a member function of vector and a global function. The global one is particularly useful for arrays (C-style arrays, not std::array) because they cannot have member functions.

So begin() returns an iterator that you can think of as a pointer: in the case of a vector, it has similar mechanics. For example, you can dereference the iterator to print the actual name:

```
1   cout << "first name is " << *it << "\n";
2   // first name is john
```

The iterator that we are given knows how to *advance*, that is, move to point to the next element. It's important to realize that the ++ refers to the idea of moving forward, that is, it is *not* the same as a ++ for pointers where you move forward in memory (i.e., increment a memory address):

```
1   ++it; // now points to jane
```

We can also use the iterator (same way as a pointer) to modify the element it points to:

```
1   it->append(" goodall"s);
2   cout << "full name is " << *it << "\n";
3   // full name is jane goodall
```

Now, the counterpart to begin() is, of course, end(), but it doesn't point to the last element—instead, it points to the element *after* the last one. Here's a clumsy illustration:

```
1               1 2 3 4
2   begin() ^        ^ end()
```

You can use end() as the terminating condition. For example, let's print the rest of those names using our it iterator variable:

```
1   while (++it != names.end())
2   {
3     cout << "another name: " << *it << "\n";
4   }
5   // another name: jill
6   // another name: jack
```

In addition to begin() and end(), we also have rbegin() and rend(), which allow us to move backward through the collection. In this case, as you may have guessed, rbegin() points to the last element and rend() to one-before-the-first:

```
1   for (auto ri = rbegin(names); ri != rend(names); ++ri)
2   {
3     cout << *ri;
4     if (ri + 1 != rend(names)) // iterator arithmetic
5       cout << ", ";
6   }
7   cout << endl;
8   // jack, jill, jane goodall, john
```

There are two things worth pointing out in the preceding. First, even though we are going through the vector backward, we still use the ++ operator on the iterator. Second, we are allowed to do arithmetic: again, when I write ri + 1, this refers to the element *just before* ri and not after.

We can also have constant iterators that do not allow modification of the object: they are returned through cbegin()/cend() and, of course, there are reverse varieties crbegin()/crend() too:

```
1   vector<string>::const_reverse_iterator jack = crbegin(names);
2   // won't work
3   *jack += "reacher";
```

Finally, it's worth mentioning the Modern C++ construct, a *range-based for loop* that serves as a shorthand for iterating all the way from a container's begin() until we reach its end():

```
1    for (auto& name : names)
2      cout << "name = " << name << "\n";
```

Notice that the iterator is automatically dereferenced here: the variable name is a reference, but you could equally iterate by value.

Traversing a Binary Tree

Let's go through the classic "comp sci" exercise of traversing a binary tree. First of all, we shall define a node of this tere as follows:

```
1    template <typename T> struct Node
2    {
3      T value;
4      Node<T> *left = nullptr;
5      Node<T> *right = nullptr;
6      Node<T> *parent = nullptr;
7      BinaryTree<T>* tree = nullptr;
8    };
```

Each node has a reference to its left and right branches, its parent (if it has one), and also to the entire tree. A node can be constructed either on its own or with a specification of its children:

```
1    explicit Node(const T& value)
2      : value(value)
3    {
4    }
5
```

```
6    Node(const T& value, Node<T>* const left, Node<T>*
     const right)
7      : value(value),
8        left(left),
9        right(right)
10   {
11     this->left->tree = this->right->tree = tree;
12     this->left->parent = this->right->parent = this;
13   }
```

Finally, we introduce a utility member function to set the tree pointer. This is done recursively accross all of the Node's children:

```
1    void set_tree(BinaryTree<T>* t)
2    {
3      tree = t;
4      if (left) left->set_tree(t);
5      if (right) right->set_tree(t);
6    }
```

Armed with this, we can now define a structure called BinaryTree—it is precisely this structure that will permit iteration:

```
1    template <typename T> struct BinaryTree
2    {
3      Node<T>* root = nullptr;
4
5      explicit BinaryTree(Node<T>* const root)
6        : root{ root }
7      {
8        root->set_tree(this);
9      }
10   };
```

Now we can define an iterator for the tree. There are three common ways of iterating a binary tree, and the one we'll implement first is preorder:

- We return the element as soon as it is encountered.

- We recursively traverse the left subtree.

- We recursively traverse the right subtree.

So let's start with a constructor:

```
1   template <typename U>
2   struct PreOrderIterator
3   {
4     Node<U>* current;
5
6     explicit PreOrderIterator(Node<U>* current)
7       : current(current)
8     {
9     }
10
11    // other members here
12  };
```

We need to define operator != to compare with other iterators. Since our iterator acts as a pointer, this is trivial:

```
1   bool operator!=(const PreOrderIterator<U>& other)
2   {
3     return current != other.current;
4   }
```

We also need the * operator for dereferencing:

```
1   Node<U>& operator*() { return *current; }
```

Now, here comes the hard part: traversing the tree. The challenge here is that we cannot make the algorithm recursive—remember, traversal happens in the ++ operator, so we end up implementing it as follows:

```
1   PreOrderIterator<U>& operator++()
2   {
3     if (current->right)
4     {
5       current = current->right;
6       while (current->left)
7         current = current->left;
8     }
9     else
10    {
11      Node<T>* p = current->parent;
12      while (p && current == p->right)
13      {
14        current = p;
15        p = p->parent;
16      }
17      current = p;
18    }
19    return *this;
20  }
```

This is quite messy! And furthermore, it looks nothing like the classic implementation of tree traveral, precisely because we don't have recursion. We'll get back to that in a while.

Now, the final question is how we expose the iterator from our
BinaryTree. If we were to define it as the *default* iterator for the tree, we
could populate its members as follows:

```
1    typedef PreOrderIterator<T> iterator;
2
3    iterator begin()
4    {
5      Node<T>* n = root;
6
7      if (n)
8        while (n->left)
9          n = n->left;
10     return iterator{ n };
11   }
12
13   iterator end()
14   {
15     return iterator{ nullptr };
16   }
```

It's worth noting that, in begin() iteration doesn't start from the root of
the entire tree; instead, it starts from the leftmost available node.

Now that all the pieces are in place, here is how we would do the
traversal:

```
1    BinaryTree<string> family{
2      new Node<string>{"me",
3        new Node<string>{"mother",
4          new Node<string>{"mother's mother"},
5          new Node<string>{"mother's father"}
6        },
7        new Node<string>{"father"}
8      }
```

```
 9   };
10
11   for (auto it = family.begin(); it != family.end(); ++it)
12   {
13     cout << (*it).value << "\n";
14   }
```

You could also expose this form of traversal as a separate object, that is:

```
1   class pre_order_traversal
2   {
3     BinaryTree<T>& tree;
4   public:
5     pre_order_traversal(BinaryTree<T>& tree) : tree{tree} {}
6     iterator begin() { return tree.begin(); }
7     iterator end() { return tree.end(); }
8   } pre_order;
```

to be used as:

```
1   for (const auto& it: family.pre_order)
2   {
3     cout << it.value << "\n";
4   }
```

Similarly, one could define in_order and post_order traversal algorithms to expose appropriate iterators.

Iteration with Coroutines

We have a serious problem: in our traversal code, operator++ is an unreadable mess that doesn't match anything you'd read about tree traversal on Wikipedia. It works, but it only works because we preinitialize the iterator to start at the leftmost node instead of the root node, which is also, shall we say, problematic and confusing.

Why do we have this problem? Because the function for the ++ operator is not resumable: it cannot keep its stack between calls, and as a result, recursion is impossible. Now, what if we had a mechanism to have our cake and eat it too: resumable functions that can perform proper recursion? Well, that's exactly what *coroutines* are for.

With coroutines, we can implement postorder tree traversal as follows:

```
1    generator<Node<T>*> post_order_impl(Node<T>* node)
2    {
3      if (node)
4      {
5        for (auto x : post_order_impl(node->left))
6          co_yield x;
7        for (auto y : post_order_impl(node->right))
8          co_yield y;
9          co_yield node;
10     }
11   }
12
13   generator<Node<T>*> post_order()
14   {
15     return post_order_impl(root);
16   }
```

Isn't this great? The algorithm is finally readable again! Furthermore, there's no begin()/end() in sight: we simply return a generator, which is a type specifically design to progressively return values that are fed to it with co_yield. After each of the values is yielded, we can suspend execution and do something else (say, print the value), then resume the iteration without losing the context. This is what makes recursion possible and allows us to write this:

```
1    for (auto it: family.post_order())
2    {
3      cout << it->value << endl;
4    }
```

Coroutines are the future of C++ and solve lots of problems for which conventional iterators are either ugly or unsuitable.

Summary

The Iterator design pattern is omnipresent in C++ in both explicit and implicit (e.g., range-based) forms. Different types of iterators exist for iterating different objects: for example, reverse iterators might apply to a vector, but not to a singly linked list.

Implementing your own iterator is as simple as providing the ++ and != operators. Most iterators are simply pointer façades and are meant to be used to traverse the collection once before they are thrown away.

Coroutines fix some of the issues present in iterators: they allow state to be preserved between calls—something that other languages (e.g., C#) have implemented a long time ago. As a consequence, coroutines allow us to write recursive algorithms.

CHAPTER 17

Mediator

A large proportion of the code we write has different components
(classes) communicating with one another through direct references or
pointers. However, there are situations when you don't want objects to be
necessarily aware of each other's presence. Or, perhaps you *do* want them
to be aware of one another, but you still don't want them to communicate
through pointers or references because, well, those can go stale and you
don't want to dereference a `nullptr`, do you?

So the Mediator is a mechanism for facilitating communication
between the components. Naturally, the mediator itself needs to be
accessible to every component taking part, which means it should either
be a global `static` variable or, alternatively, just a reference that gets
injected into every component.

Chat Room

Your typical internet chat room is the classic example of the Mediator
design pattern, so let's implement this before we move on to the more
complicated stuff.

© Dmitri Nesteruk 2018
D. Nesteruk, *Design Patterns in Modern C++*, https://doi.org/10.1007/978-1-4842-3603-1_17

The most trivial implementation of a participant in a chat room can be as simple as:

```
1   struct Person
2   {
3     string name;
4     ChatRoom* room = nullptr;
5     vector<string> chat_log;
6
7     Person(const string& name);
8
9     void receive(const string& origin, const string& message);
10    void say(const string& message) const;
11    void pm(const string& who, const string& message) const;
12  };
```

So we've got a person with a name (user id), a chat log, and a pointer to the actual ChatRoom. We have a constructor and then three member functions:

- receive() allows us to receive a message. Typically what this function would do is show the message on the user's screen, and also add it to the chat log.

- say() allows the person to broadcast a message to everyone in the room.

- pm() is private messaging functionality. You need to specify the name of the person the message is intended for.

Both say() and pm() just relay operations to the chatroom. Speaking of which, let's actually implement ChatRoom—it's not particularly complicated:

```
1    struct ChatRoom
2    {
3      vector<Person*> people; // assume append-only
4
5      void join(Person* p);
6      void broadcast(const string& origin, const
         string& message);
7      void message(const string& origin, const string& who,
8        const string& message);
9    };
```

Whether to use pointers, references, or a shared_ptr for actually storing a list of chat room participants is ultimately up to you: the only restriction is that an std::vector cannot store references. So, I have decided to go with pointers here. The ChatRoom API is very simple:

- join() gets a person to join the room. We are not going to implement leave(), instead deferring the idea to a subsequent example in this chapter.

- broadcast() sends the message to everyone... well, not quite everyone: we don't need to send the message back to the person who sent it.

- message() sends a private message.

The implementation of join() is as follows:

```
1   void ChatRoom::join(Person* p)
2   {
3     string join_msg = p->name + " joins the chat";
4     broadcast("room", join_msg);
5     p->room = this;
6     people.push_back(p);
7   }
```

Just like a classic IRC chatroom, we broadcast the message that someone has joined to everyone in the room. The origin in this case is specified as "room" rather than the person who's joined. We then set the person's room pointer and add them to the list of people in the room.

Now, let's look at broadcast(): this is where a message is sent to every room participant. Remember, each participant has his or her own Person::receive() function for processing the message, so the implementation is somewhat trivial:

```
1   void ChatRoom::broadcast(const string& origin, const
    string& message)
2   {
3     for (auto p : people)
4       if (p->name != origin)
5         p->receive(origin, message);
6   }
```

Whether or not we want to prevent a broadcast message to be relayed to ourselves is a point of debate, but I'm actively avoiding it here. Everyone else gets the message, though.

Finally, here's private messaging implemented with message():

```
1    void ChatRoom::message(const string& origin,
2      const string& who, const string& message)
3    {
4      auto target = find_if(begin(people), end(people),
5        [&](const Person* p) { return p->name == who; });
6      if (target != end(people))
7      {
8        (*target)->receive(origin, message);
9      }
10   }
```

This searches for the recepient in the list of people and, if the recepient is found (because who knows, they could have left the room), dispatches the message to that person.

Coming back to Person's implementations of say() and pm(), here they are:

```
1    void Person::say(const string& message) const
2    {
3      room->broadcast(name, message);
4    }
5
6    void Person::pm(const string& who, const string& message) const
7    {
8      room->message(name, who, message);
9    }
```

As for receive(), well, this is a good place to actually display the message on-screen as well as add it to the chat log.

```
1   void Person::receive(const string& origin, const
    string& message)
2   {
3     string s{ origin + ": \"" + message + "\"" };
4     cout << "[" << name << "'s chat session] " << s << "\n";
5     chat_log.emplace_back(s);
6   }
```

We go the extra mile here by displaying not just who the message came from, but whose chat session we're currently in—this will be useful for diagnosing who said what and when.

Here's the scenario that we'll run through:

```
1    ChatRoom room;
2
3    Person john{ "john" };
4    Person jane{ "jane" };
5    room.join(&john);
6    room.join(&jane);
7    john.say("hi room");
8    jane.say("oh, hey john");
9
10   Person simon("simon");
11   room.join(&simon);
12   simon.say("hi everyone!");
13
14   jane.pm("simon", "glad you could join us, simon");
```

and here is the output:

```
1   [john's chat session] room: "jane joins the chat"
2   [jane's chat session] john: "hi room"
3   [john's chat session] jane: "oh, hey john"
4   [john's chat session] room: "simon joins the chat"
5   [jane's chat session] room: "simon joins the chat"
6   [john's chat session] simon: "hi everyone!"
7   [jane's chat session] simon: "hi everyone!"
8   [simon's chat session] jane: "glad you could join us, simon"
```

Mediator with Events

In the chat room example, we've encountered a consistent theme: the participants need notification whenever someone posts a message. This seems like a perfect scenario for the Observer pattern, which is discussed in Chapter 20: the idea of the mediator having an event that is shared by all participants; participants can then subscribe to the event to receive notifications, and they can also cause the event to fire, thus triggering said notifications.

Events are not built into C++ (unlike, e.g., C#), so we'll use a library solution for this demo. Boost.Signals2 offers us the requisite functionality, albeit with a slightly different terminology: we typically speak of *signals* (objects that generate a notification) and *slots* (functions that handle notifications).

Instead of redoing the chat room once again, let's go for a simpler example: imagine a game of football (soccer), with players and a football coach. When coaches see their team scoring, they naturally want to congratulate the player. Of course, they need some information about the event, like *who* scored the goal and how many goals they have scored so far.

We can introduce a base class for any sort of event data:

```
1    struct EventData
2    {
3      virtual ~EventData() = default;
4      virtual void print() const = 0;
5    };
```

I've added the print() function so that each event can be printed to the command line, and also a virtual destructor to make ReSharper shut up about it. Now, we can derive from this class in order to store some goal-related data:

```
1    struct PlayerScoredData : EventData
2    {
3      string player_name;
4      int goals_scored_so_far;
5
6      PlayerScoredData(const string& player_name, const int
         goals_scored_so_far)
7        : player_name(player_name),
8          goals_scored_so_far(goals_scored_so_far) {}
9
10     void print() const override
11     {
12       cout << player_name << " has scored! (their "
13         << goals_scored_so_far << " goal)" << "\n";
14     }
15   };
```

We are once again going to build a mediator, but it will have *no* behaviors! Seriously, with an event-driven infrastructure, they are no longer needed:

```
1   struct Game
2   {
3     signal<void(EventData*)> events; // observer
4   };
```

In fact, you could get away with just having a global signal and not make a Game class at all, but we are using the principle of least surprise here, and if a Game& is injected into a component, we know there's a clear dependency there.

Anyways, we can now construct the Player class. A player has a name, the number of goals they scored during the match, and a reference to the mediator Game, of course:

```
1   struct Player
2   {
3     string name;
4     int goals_scored = 0;
5     Game& game;
6
7     Player(const string& name, Game& game)
8       : name(name), game(game) {}
9
10    void score()
11    {
12      goals_scored++;
13      PlayerScoredData ps{name, goals_scored};
14      game.events(&ps);
15    }
16  };
```

The Player::score() is the interesting function here: it uses the events signal to create a PlayerScoredData and post it for all subscribers to see. Who gets this event? Why, a Coach, of course:

```
1    struct Coach
2    {
3      Game& game;
4      explicit Coach(Game& game) : game(game)
5      {
6        // celebrate if player has scored <3 goals
7        game.events.connect([](EventData* e)
8        {
9          PlayerScoredData* ps = dynamic_cast
             <PlayerScoredData*>(e);
10         if (ps && ps->goals_scored_so_far < 3)
11         {
12           cout << "coach says: well done, " << ps->player_
               name << "\n";
13         }
14       });
15     }
16   };
```

The implementation of the Coach class is trivial; our coach doesn't even get a name. But we do give him a constructor where a subscription is created to game.events such that, whenever something happens, the coach gets to process the event data in the provided lambda (slot).

Notice that the argument type of the lambda is EventData*—we don't know if a player has scored or has been sent off, so we need dynamic_cast (or a similar mechanism) to determine we've got the right type.

The interesting thing is that all the magic happens at the set-up stage: there's no need to explicitly enlist slots for a particular signal. The client is free to create objects using their constructors and then, when the player scores, the notifications are sent:

```
1   Game game;
2   Player player{ "Sam", game };
3   Coach coach{ game };
4
5   player.score();
6   player.score();
7   player.score(); // ignored by coach
```

This procudes the following output:

```
1   coach says: well done, Sam
2   coach says: well done, Sam
```

The output is only two lines long because, on the third goal, the coach isn't impressed anymore.

Summary

The Mediator design pattern essentially proposes an introduction of an in-between component that everyone in a system has a reference to and can use to communicate with one another. Instead of direct memory addresses, communication can happen through identifiers (usernames, unique IDs, etc).

The simplest implementation of a mediator is a member list and a function that goes through the list and does what it's intended to do—whether on every element of the list or selectively.

A more sophisticated implementation of Mediator can use events to allow participants to subscribe (and unsubscribe) to things happening in the system. This way, messages sent from one component to another can be treated as events. In this set-up, it is also easy for participants to unsubscribe to certain events if they are no longer interested in them or if they are about to leave the system altogether.

CHAPTER 18

Memento

When we looked at the Command design pattern, we noted that recording a list of every single change theoretically allows you to roll back the system to any point in time—after all, you've kept a record of all the modifications.

Sometimes, though, you don't really care about playing back the state of the system, but you *do* care about being able to roll back the system to a *particular* state, if need be.

This is precisely what the Memento pattern does: it stores the state of the system and returns it as a dedicated, read-only object with no behavior of its own. This "token," if you will, can be used only for feeding it back into the system to restore it to the state it represents.

Let's look at an example.

Bank Account

Let's use an example of a bank account that we've made before:

```
1   class BankAccount
2   {
3     int balance = 0;
4   public:
5     explicit BankAccount(const int balance)
6       : balance(balance) {}
```

© Dmitri Nesteruk 2018
D. Nesteruk, *Design Patterns in Modern C++*, https://doi.org/10.1007/978-1-4842-3603-1_18

but now we decide to make a bank account with only a deposit() function. Instead of it being void as in previous examples, deposit() will now be made to return a Memento:

```
1    Memento deposit(int amount)
2    {
3      balance += amount;
4      return { balance };
5    }
```

and the Memento will then be usable for rolling back the account to the previous state:

```
1      void restore(const Memento& m)
2      {
3        balance = m.balance;
4      }
5    };
```

As for the memento itself, we can go for a trivial implementation:

```
1    class Memento
2    {
3      int balance;
4    public:
5      Memento(int balance)
6        : balance(balance)
7      {
8      }
9      friend class BankAccount;
10   };
```

There are two things to point out here:

- The Memento class is immutable. Imagine if you *could*, in fact, change the balance: you could roll back the account to a state it was never in!

- The memento declares BankAccount as a friend class. This allows the account to actually use the balance field. An alternative that would also have worked is to make Memento an inner class of BankAccount.

And here is how one would go about using such a set-up:

```
1    void memento()
2    {
3      BankAccount ba{ 100 };
4      auto m1 = ba.deposit(50);
5      auto m2 = ba.deposit(25);
6      cout << ba << "\n"; // Balance: 175
7
8      // undo to m1
9      ba.restore(m1);
10     cout << ba << "\n"; // Balance: 150
11
12     // redo
13     ba.restore(m2);
14     cout << ba << "\n"; // Balance: 175
15   }
```

This implementation is good enough, through there are some things missing. For example, you never get a Memento representing the opening balance because a constructor cannot return a value. You could stick a pointer in there, but it seems a bit ugly.

Undo and Redo

What if you were to store *every* Memento generated by BankAccount?
In this case, you'd have a situation similar to our implementation of the
Command pattern, where undo and redo operations are a byproduct of
this recording. Let's see how we can get undo/redo functionality with a
Memento.

We'll introduce a new bank account class, BankAccount2, that's going
to keep hold of every single Memento it ever generates:

```
1   class BankAccount2 // supports undo/redo
2   {
3     int balance = 0;
4     vector<shared_ptr<Memento>> changes;
5     int current;
6   public:
7     explicit BankAccount2(const int balance) :
      balance(balance)
8     {
9       changes.emplace_back(make_shared<Memento>(balance));
10      current = 0;
11    }
```

We have now solved the problem of returning to the initial balance:
the memento for the initial change is stored as well. Of course, this
memento isn't actually returned, so in order to roll back to it, well, I
suppose you could implement some reset() function or something—it's
totally up to you.

In the preceding, we are using shared_ptr to store the mementos, and
we also use shared_ptr to return them. Furthermore, we are using the
current field as a "pointer" into the list of changes, so that if we do decide
to undo and move back a step, we can always redo and revert to something
we just had.

Now, here's the implementation of the deposit() function:

```
1   shared_ptr<Memento> deposit(int amount)
2   {
3     balance += amount;
4     auto m = make_shared<Memento>(balance);
5     changes.push_back(m);
6     ++current;
7     return m;
8   }
```

Now here comes the fun stuff (we're still listing members of
BankAccount2, by the way). We add a method to restore the account state
based on a memento:

```
1   void restore(const shared_ptr<Memento>& m)
2   {
3     if (m)
4     {
5       balance = m->balance;
6       changes.push_back(m);
7       current = changes.size() - 1;
8     }
9   }
```

The restoration process is significantly different to the one we've
looked at earlier. First, we actually check that the shared_ptr is
initialized—this is relevant because we now have a way of signaling
no-ops: just return a default value. Also, when we restore a memento, we
actually push that memento into the list of changes so an undo operation
will work correctly on it.

Now, here is the (rather tricky) implementation of undo():

```
1   shared_ptr<Memento> undo()
2   {
3     if (current > 0)
4     {
5       --current;
6       auto m = changes[current];
7       balance = m->balance;
8       return m;
9     }
10    return{};
11  }
```

We can only undo() if current points to a change that is great than zero. If that's the case, we move the pointer back, grab the change at that position, apply it and then return that change. If we cannot roll back to a previous memento, we return a default-constructed shared_ptr, for which we check in restore().

The implementation of redo() is very similar:

```
1   shared_ptr<Memento> redo()
2   {
3     if (current + 1 < changes.size())
4     {
5       ++current;
6       auto m = changes[current];
7       balance = m->balance;
8       return m;
9     }
10    return{};
11  }
```

Again, we need to be able to redo something: if we can, we do it safely, if not—we do nothing and return an empty pointer. Putting it all together, we can now start using the undo/redo functionality:

```
1   BankAccount2 ba{ 100 };
2   ba.deposit(50);
3   ba.deposit(25); // 125
4   cout << ba << "\n";
5
6   ba.undo();
7   cout << "Undo 1: " << ba << "\n"; // Undo 1: 150
8   ba.undo();
9   cout << "Undo 2: " << ba << "\n"; // Undo 2: 100
10  ba.redo();
11  cout << "Redo 2: " << ba << "\n"; // Redo 2: 150
12  ba.undo(); // back to 100 again
```

Summary

The Memento pattern is all about handing out tokens that can be used to restore the system to a prior state. Typically, the token contains all the information necessary to move the system to a particular state, and if it's small enough, you can also use it to record *all* the states of the system so as to allow not just the arbitrary resetting of the system to a prior state, but controlled navigation backward (undo) and forward (redo) of all the states the system was in.

CHAPTER 19

Null Object

We don't always choose the interfaces we work with. For example, I'd rather have my car drive me to my destination by itself, without me having to give 100% of my attention to the road and the dangerous lunatics driving next to me. And it's the same with software: sometimes you don't really want a piece of functionality, but it's built into the interface. So what do you do? You make a Null Object.

Scenario

Suppose you inherited a library that uses the following interface:

```
1  struct Logger
2  {
3    virtual ~Logger() = default;
4    virtual void info(const string& s) = 0;
5    virtual void warn(const string& s) = 0;
6  };
```

The library uses this interface to operate on bank accounts such as:

```
1  struct BankAccount
2  {
3    std::shared_ptr<Logger> log;
4    string name;
5    int balance = 0;
6
```

© Dmitri Nesteruk 2018
D. Nesteruk, *Design Patterns in Modern C++*, https://doi.org/10.1007/978-1-4842-3603-1_19

```
7      BankAccount(const std::shared_ptr<Logger>& logger,
8        const string& name, int balance)
9          : log{logger}, name{name}, balance{balance} { }
10
11     // more members here
12   };
```

In fact, BankAccount can have member functions similar to:

```
1    void BankAccount::deposit(int amount)
2    {
3      balance += amount;
4      log->info("Deposited $" + lexical_cast<string>(amount)
5        + " to " + name + ", balance is now $" + lexical_
         cast<string>(balance));
6    }
```

So, what's the problem here? Well, if you *do* need logging, there's no problem, you just implement your own logging class...

```
1    struct ConsoleLogger : Logger
2    {
3      void info(const string& s) override
4      {
5        cout << "INFO: " << s << endl;
6      }
7
8      void warn(const string& s) override
9      {
10       cout << "WARNING!!! " << s << endl;
11     }
12   };
```

and you can use it straight away. But what if you *don't want logging at all*?

Null Object

Look at BankAccount's constructor once again:

```
1   BankAccount(const shared_ptr<Logger>& logger,
2       const string& name, int balance)
```

Since the constructor takes a logger, it is *unsafe* to assume that you can get away with just passing it an uninitialized shared_ptr <BankAccount>(). BankAccount *could* be checking the pointer internally before dispatching on it, but you don't know that it does, and without extra documentation it's impossible to tell.

As a consequence, the only thing that would be reasonable to pass into BankAccount is a null object—a class which conforms to the interface but contains no functionality:

```
1   struct NullLogger : Logger
2   {
3     void info(const string& s) override {}
4     void warn(const string& s) override {}
5   };
```

shared_ptr is *not* a Null Object

It's important to note that shared_ptr and other smart pointer classes are *not* null objects. A null object is something that preserves correct operation (does a no-op). But invocations on an uninitialized smart pointers crash and burn:

```
1   shared_ptr<int> n;
2   int x = *n + 1; // yikes!
```

What's interesting to note is that there is no way of making smart pointers "safe" from the perspective of invocation. In other words, you cannot write such a smart pointer where `foo->bar()` would magically become a no-op if `foo` is uninitialized. The reason for this is both the prefix `*` and postfix `->` operators simply proxy the underlying (raw) pointer over. And there's no way of doing a no-op on a pointer.

Design Improvements

Stop and think for a moment: if `BankAccount` was under your control, could you improve the interface such that it is easier to use? Well, here are some ideas:

- Put pointer checks everywhere. This sorts out the correctness on the `BankAccount`'s end, but doesn't stop getting library users confused. Remember, you're still not communicating that the pointer can be null.

- Add a default argument value, something like `const shared_ptr<Logger>& logger = no_logging` where `no_logging` is, say, some member of the `BankAccount` class. Even if this is the case, you would still have to perform checks on the pointer value in every location where you want to use the object.

- Use the `optional` type. This is idiomatically correct and communicates intent, but leads to the horror of passing in an `optional<shared_ptr<T>>` and the subsequent check of whether an optional is empty or not.

Implicit Null Object

There's another radical idea, which involves a double-hop around the Logger bend. It involves subdividing the process of logging into invocation (we want a nice Logger interface) and operation (what the logger actually does). So consider the following:

```
1   struct OptionalLogger : Logger {
2     shared_ptr<Logger> impl;
3     static shared_ptr<Logger> no_logging;
4     Logger(const shared_ptr<Logger>& logger) : impl{logger} {}
5     virtual void info(const string& s) override {
6       if (impl) impl->info(s); // null check here
7     }
8     // and similar checks for other members
9   };
10
11  // a static instance of a null object
12  shared_ptr<Logger> BankAccount::no_logging{};
```

So now we've abstracted away invocation from implementation. What we do now is redefine the BankAccount constructor as follows:

```
1   shared_ptr<OptionalLogger> logger;
2   BankAccount(const string& name, int balance,
3     const shared_ptr<Logger>& logger = no_logging)
4     : log{make_shared<OptionalLogger>(logger)},
5       name{name},
6       balance{balance} { }
```

As you can see, there's clever subterfuge here: we are taking a Logger but storing an OptionalLogger (this is the Proxy design pattern). Then, all the calls to this optional logger are safe—they only 'happen' if underlying object is available:

```
1   BankAccount account{ "primary account", 1000 };
2   account.deposit(2000); // no crash
```

The proxy object that is implemented in the preceding example is essentially a customized version of the Pimpl idiom.

Summary

The Null Object pattern raises an issue of API design: what kinds of assumptions can we make about the objects we depend upon? If we are taking a pointer (raw or smart), do we then have an obligation to check this pointer on every use?

If you feel no such obligation, then the only way the client can implement a Null Object is to contruct a no-op implementation of the required interface and pass that instance in. That said, this only works well with functions: if the object's fields are also being used, for example, then you are in real trouble.

If you want to proactively support the idea of Null Objects being passed as arguments, you need to be explicit about it: either specify the parameter type as std::optional, give the parameter a default value that hints at a built-in Null Object (e.g., = no_logging), or just write documentation that explains what kind of value is expected at this location.

CHAPTER 20

Observer

The observer pattern is a popular and necessary pattern, so it is surprising that, unlike other languages (e.g., C#), neither C++ nor the Standard Library come with a ready-to-use implementation. Nonetheless, a safe, properly implemented observer (if there can be such a thing) is a technically sophisticated construct, so in this chapter we'll investigate it with all its gory details.

Property Observers

People get old. It's a fact of life. But when someone gets older by a year we might want to congratulate them on their birthday. But how? Given a definition such as:

```
1   struct Person
2   {
3     int age;
4     Person(int age) : age{age} {}
5   };
```

How do we know when a person's age changes? We don't. To see changes, we could try polling: reading a person's age every 100 milliseconds and comparing the new value with the previous. This approach will work, but is tedious and does not scale. We need to be smarter about this.

© Dmitri Nesteruk 2018
D. Nesteruk, *Design Patterns in Modern C++*, https://doi.org/10.1007/978-1-4842-3603-1_20

We know that we want to be informed on every *write* to a person's age field. Well, the only way to catch this is to make a setter, that is:

```
1    struct Person
2    {
3      int get_age() const { return age; }
4      void set_age(const int value) { age = value; }
5    private:
6      int age;
7    };
```

The setter set_age() is where we can notify whoever cares that age has, in fact, changed. But how?

Observer<T>

Well, one approach is to define some sort of base class that would need to be inherited by anyone interested in getting Person's changes:

```
1    struct PersonListener
2    {
3      virtual void person_changed(Person& p,
4        const string& property_name, const any new_value) = 0;
5    };
```

However, this approach is quite stifling, because property changes can occur on types other than Person and we would not want to spawn additional classes for those too. Here's something a little more generic:

```
1    template<typename T> struct Observer
2    {
3      virtual void field_changed(T& source, const string&
       field_name) = 0;
4    };
```

The two parameters in `field_changed()` are, hopefully, self-explanatory. The first is a reference to the object whose field actually changed, the second is the name of the field. Yes, the name is passed as a `string`, which does hurt the refactorability of our code (what if the field name changes?).[1]

This implementation would allow us to observe changes to a `Person` class and, for example, write them to the command line:

```
1   struct ConsolePersonObserver : Observer<Person>
2   {
3     void field_changed(Person& source, const string&
      field_name) override
4     {
5       cout << "Person's " << field_name << " has changed to "
6             << source.get_age() << ".\n";
7     }
8   };
```

The flexibility we introduced into the scenario would allow us, for example, to observe property changes on multiple classes. For instance, if we add class `Creature` to the mix, you can now observe on both:

```
1   struct ConsolePersonObserver : Observer<Person>,
              Observer<Creature>
2   {
3     void field_changed(Person& source, ...) { ... }
4     void field_changed(Creature& source, ...) { ... }
5   };
```

---

[1]C# has explicitly solved this problem *twice* in successive releases. First, it introduced an attribute called `[CallerMemberName]` that inserted the name of calling function/property as the string value of a parameter. A second release simply introduced `nameof(Foo)`, which would take the name of a symbol and turn it into a string.

Another alternative is to use std::any and do away with a generic implementation. Try it!

Observable<T>

So anyways, let's get back to Person. Since this is about to become an observable class, it would have to take on new responsibilities, namely:

- Keeping a private list of all the observers interested in Person's changes

- Letting the observers subscribe()/unsubscribe() to changes in Person

- Informing all observers when a change is actually made with notify()

All of this functionality can quite happily be moved to a separate base class so as to avoid replicating it for every potential observable:

```
1   template <typename T> struct Observable
2   {
3     void notify(T& source, const string& name) { ... }
4     void subscribe(Observer<T>* f) { observers.push_back(f); }
5     void unsubscribe(Observer<T>* f) { ... }
6   private:
7     vector<Observer<T>*> observers;
8   };
```

We have implemented subscribe()—it just adds a new observer to the private list of observers. The list of observers isn't available to anyone—not even to the derived class. We don't want people arbitrarily manipulating this collection.

Next up, we need to implement notify(). The idea is simple: go through every observer and invoke its field_changed() one after another:

```
1   void notify(T& source, const string& name)
2   {
3     for (auto obs : observers)
4       obs->field_changed(source, name);
5   }
```

It's not enough to inherit from Observable<T>, though: our class also needs to put do its part in calling notify() whenever a field is changed.

Consider the setter set_age(), for example. It now has three responsibilities:

- Check that the name has actually changed. If age is 20 and we are assigning 20 to it, there is no point performing any assignment or notification.

- Assign the field to the appropriate value.

- Call notify() with the right arguments.

Consequently, the new implementation of set_age() would look something like the following:

```
1    struct Person : Observable<Person>
2    {
3      void set_age(const int age)
4      {
5        if (this->age == age) return;
6        this->age = age;
7        notify(*this, "age");
8      }
9    private:
10     int age;
11   };
```

Connecting Observers and Observables

We are now ready to start using the infrastructure we created in order to get notification on Person's field changes (well, we could call them *properties*, really). Here's a reminder of what our observer looks like:

```
1    struct ConsolePersonObserver : Observer<Person>
2    {
3      void field_changed(Person& source,
4        const string& field_name) override
5      {
6        cout << "Person's " << field_name << " has
                  changed to "
7             << source.get_age() << ".\n";
8      }
9    };
```

And here is how we use it:

```
1    Person p{ 20 };
2    ConsolePersonObserver cpo;
3    p.subscribe(&cpo);
4    p.set_age(21); // Person's age has changed to 21.
5    p.set_age(22); // Person's age has changed to 22.
```

So long as you don't concern yourself with issues around property dependencies and thread safety/reentrancy, you can stop here, take this implementation, and start using it. If you want to see discussions of more sophisticated approaches, read on.

Dependency Problems

People aged 16 or older (could be different in your country) can vote. So suppose we want to be notified of changes to a person's voting rights. First, let's assume that our Person type has the following getter:

```
1    bool get_can_vote() const { return age >= 16; }
```

Note that get_can_vote() has no backing field and no setter (we *could* introduce such a field, but it would be self-evidently redundant), yet we also feel obliged to notify() on it. But how? Well, we could try to find what *causes* can_vote to change… that's right, set_age() does! So if we want notifications on changes in voting status, these need to be done in set_age(). Get ready, you're in for a surprise!

```
1    void set_age(int value) const
2    {
3      if (age == value) return;
4
5      auto old_can_vote = can_vote(); // store old value
6      age = value;
7      notify(*this, "age");
8
9      if (old_can_vote != can_vote()) // check value has
                                                 changed
10         notify(*this, "can_vote");
11   }
```

There's far too much in the preceding function. Not only do we check if age has changed, we also check that can_vote has changed and notify on it too! You can probably guess this approach doesn't scale well, right? Imagine can_vote being dependent on *two* fields, say age and citizenship—it means both of their setters have to handle can_vote notifications. And what if age also affects ten other properties this way?

This is an unworkable solution that would lead to brittle code that's impossible to maintain, since relationships between variables need to be tracked manually.

Speaking plainly, in the preceding scenario, can_vote is a *dependent property* of age. The challenge of dependent properties is essentially the challenge of tools such as Excel: given lots of dependencies between different cells, how do you know which cells to recalculate when one of them changes.

Property dependencies *can*, of course, be formalized into some sort of map<string, vector<string>> that would keep a list of properties affected by a property (or, inversely, all the properties that affect a property). The sad thing is that this map would have to be defined by hand, and keeping it in sync with actual code is rather tricky.

Unsubscription and Thread Safety

One thing that I've neglected to discuss is how an observer might unsubscribe() from an observable. Generally, you want to remove yourself from the list of observers, which in a single-threaded scenario is as simple as:

```
1   void unsubscribe(Observer<T>* observer)
2   {
3     observers.erase(
4       remove(observers.begin(), observers.end(), observer),
5       observers.end());
6   };
```

While the use of the erase-remove idiom is technically correct, it is only correct in a single-threaded scenario. std::vector is not thread-safe, so calling, say, subscribe() and unsubscribe() at the same time could lead to unintended consequences, since both functions modify the vector.

This is easily cured: simply put a lock on all of observable's operations. This can look as simple as:

```
1    template <typename T>
2    struct Observable
3    {
4            void notify(T& source, const string& name)
5            {
6                    scoped_lock<mutex> lock{ mtx };
7                    ...
8            }
9            void subscribe(Observer<T>* f)
10           {
11                   scoped_lock<mutex> lock{ mtx };
12                   ...
13           }
14           void unsubscribe(Observer<T>* o)
15           {
16                   scoped_lock<mutex> lock{ mtx };
17                   ...
18           }
19   private:
20           vector<Observer<T>*> observers;
21           mutex mtx;
22   };
```

Another, very viable, alternative is to use something like a concurrent_ vector from TPL/PPL. Naturally you lose ordering guarantees (in other words, adding two objects one after another doesn't guarantee they are notified in that order), but it certainly saves you from having to manage locks yourself.

Reentrancy

The last implementation provides some thread safety through locking any of the three key methods when ever someone needs it. But now let's imagine the following scenario: you have a TrafficAdministration component that keeps monitoring a person until they're old enough to drive. When they're 17, the component unsubscribes:

```
1   struct TrafficAdministration : Observer<Person>
2   {
3     void TrafficAdministration::field_changed(
4       Person& source, const string& field_name) override
5     {
6       if (field_name == "age")
7       {
8         if (source.get_age() < 17)
9           cout << "Whoa there, you are not old enough to
              drive!\n";
10        else
11        {
12          // oh, ok, they are old enough, let's not monitor
              them anymore
13          cout << "We no longer care!\n";
14          source.unsubscribe(this);
15        }
16      }
17    }
18  };
```

This is a problem because, when age turns to 17, the overall chain of calls will be:

```
1   notify() --> field_changed() --> unsubscribe()
```

This is a problem because in unsubscribe() we end up trying to take a lock that's already taken. This is a *reentrancy* problem. There are different ways to handle this.

- One way is to simply prohibit such situations. After all, at least in this particular case, it's very obvious that reentrancy is taking place here.

- Another way is to bail out on the idea of removing elements from the collection. Instead, we could go for something like:

```
1   void unsubscribe(Observer<T>* o)
2   {
3     auto it = find(observers.begin(), observers.end(), o);
4     if (it != observers.end())
5       *it = nullptr; // cannot do this for a set
6   }
```

And, subsequently, when you notify(), you just need an extra check:

```
1   void notify(T& source, const string& name)
2   {
3   for (auto obs : observers)
4     if (obs)
5       obs->field_changed(source, name);
6   }
```

Of course, the preceding only solves possible contention between notify() and subscribe(). If you were to, for example, subscribe() and unsubscribe() at the same time, that's still concurrent modification of collection—and it can still fail. So, at the very least, you might want to keep a lock there.

Yet another possibility is to just make a copy of the entire collection in notify(). You *do* need the lock still, you just don't apply it to nofications. Here's what I mean:

```
1   void notify(T& source, const string& name)
2   {
3     vector<Observer<T>*> observers_copy;
4     {
5       lock_guard<mutex_t> lock{ mtx };
6       observers_copy = observers;
7     }
8     for (auto obs : observers_copy)
9       if (obs)
10        obs->field_changed(source, name);
11  }
```

In the preceding implementation, we do take a lock but by the time we call field_changed, the lock has been released, since it's only created in the artificial scope used to copy the vector. I wouldn't worry about efficiency here, since a vector of pointers doesn't take up that much memory.

Finally, it's always possible to replace a mutex by a recursive_mutex. Generally speaking, recursive mutexes are hated by most developers (proof on SO), not just due to performance implications, but more due to the fact that in the majority of cases (just like Observer example), you can get away with using ordinary, nonrecursive variants if you design your code a bit better.

There are some interesting practical concerns that we haven't really discussed here. They include the following:

- What happens if the same observer is added twice?

- If I allow duplicate observers, does ubsubscribe() remove every single instance?

- How is the behavior affected if we use a different container? For example, we decide to prevent duplicates by using an std::set or boost::unordered_set, what does this imply for ordinary operations?

- What if I want observers that are ranked by priority?

There and other practical concerns are all manageable once your foundations are solid. We won't spend further time discussing them here.

Observer via Boost.Signals2

There are many prepackaged implementation of the Observer pattern, and probably the most well known is the Boost.Signals2 library. Essentially, this library provides a type called signal that represents a *signal* in C++ terminology (called *event* elsewhere). This signal can be subscribed to by providing a function or lambda. It can also be unsubscribed to and, when you want to notify on this, it can be fired.

Using Boost.Signals2, we can define Observer<T> as follows:

```
1  template <typename T>
2  struct Observable
3  {
4    signal<void(T&, const string&)> property_changed;
5  };
```

and its invocation looks as follows:

```
1  struct Person : Observable<Person>
2  {
3    ...
4    void set_age(const int age)
```

```
 5      {
 6          if (this->age == age) return;
 7
 8          this->age = age;
 9          property_changed(*this, "age");
10      }
11    };
```

The actual use of the API would directly use the signal unless, of course, you decided to add more API trappings to make it easier:

```
1    Person p{123};
2    auto conn = p.property_changed.connect([](Person&, const
                  string& prop_name)
3    {
4      cout << prop_name << " has been changed" << endl;
5    });
6    p.set_age(20); // name has been changed
7
8    // later, optionally
9    conn.disconnect();
```

The result of a connect() call is a connection object that can also be used to unsubscribe when you no longer need notifications from the signal.

Summary

Without a doubt, the code presented in this chapter is a clear example of overthinking and overengineering a problem way beyond what most people would want to achieve.

Let's recap the main design decisions when implementing Observer:

- Decide what information you want your observable to communicate. For example, if you are handling field/property changes, you can include the name of the property. You can also specify old/new values, but passing the type could be problematic.

- Do you want your observers to been tire classes, or are you OK with just having a list of virtual functions?

- How do you want to handle observers unsubscribing?

  - If you don't plan to support unsubscription—congratulations, you'll save a lot of effort implementing the Observer, since there are no removal issues in reentrancy scenarios.

  - If you plan to support an explicit unsubscribe() function, you probably don't want to erase-remove right in the function, but instead mark your elements for removal and remove them later.

  - If you don't like the idea of dispatching on a (posibly null) raw pointer, consider using a `weak_ptr` instead.

- Is it likely that the functions of an `Observer<T>` will be invoked from several different threads? If they are, you need to protect your subscription list:

  - You can put a `scoped_lock` on all relevant functions; or

  - You can use a thread-safe collection such as the TBB/PPL `concurrent_vector`. You lose ordering guarantees.

- Are multiple subscriptions from the same source allowed? If they are, you cannot use an `std::set`.

There is, sadly, no ideal implementation of Observer that ticks all the boxes. Whichever implementation you go for, some compromises are expected.

CHAPTER 21

State

I must confess: my behavior is governed by my state. If I didn't get enough sleep, I'm going to be a bit tired. If I had a drink, I wouldn't get behind the wheel. All of these are *states* and they govern my behavior: how I feel, and what I can and cannot do.

I can, of course, transition from one state to another. I can go get a coffee, and this will take me from sleepy to alert (I hope!). So we can think of coffee as a *trigger* that causes a transition of yours truly from sleepy to alert. Here, let me clumsily illustrate it for you:

```
1           coffee
2   sleepy --------> alert
```

So, the State design pattern is a very simple idea: state controls behavior; state can be changed; the only thing that the jury is out on is *who* triggers the state change.

There are, fundamentally, two ways:

- States are actual classes with behaviors, and these behaviors switch the actual state from one to another.

- States and transitions are just enumerations. We have a special component called a *state machine* that performs the actual transitions.

Both of these approaches are viable, but it's really the second approach that is the most common. We'll take a look at both of them, but I must admit I'll glance over the first one, since this isn't how people typically do things.

© Dmitri Nesteruk 2018
D. Nesteruk, *Design Patterns in Modern C++*, https://doi.org/10.1007/978-1-4842-3603-1_21

State-Driven State Transitions

We'll begin with the most trivial example out there: a light switch. It can only be in the *on* and *off* states. We're going to build a model where any state is capable of switching to some other state: while this reflects the "classic" implementation of the State design pattern (as per the GoF book), it's not something I'd recommend.

First, let's model the light switch: all it has is a state and some means of switching from one state to another:

```
1    class LightSwitch
2    {
3      State *state;
4    public:
5      LightSwitch()
6      {
7        state = new OffState();
8      }
9      void set_state(State* state)
10     {
11       this->state = state;
12     }
13   };
```

This all looks perfectly reasonable. We can now define the State, which in this particular case, is going to be an actual class:

```
1    struct State
2    {
3      virtual void on(LightSwitch *ls)
4      {
5        cout << "Light is already on\n";
6      }
```

```
 7     virtual void off(LightSwitch *ls)
 8     {
 9       cout << "Light is already off\n";
10     }
11   };
```

This implementation is far from intuitive, so much so that we need to discuss it slowly and carefully, because from the outset, nothing about the State class makes sense.

First of all, State is not abstract! You'd think that a state you have no way (or reason!) of reaching would be abstract. But it's not.

Second, State allows the switching from one state to another. This... to a reasonable person, it makes no sense. Imagine the light switch: it's the switch that changes states. The state itself isn't expected to change *itself*, and yet it appears this is exactly what it does.

Third, perhaps most bewildering, the default behavior of State::on/off claims that we are *already* in this state! This will come together, somewhat, as we implement the rest of the example.

We now implement the On and Off states:

```
 1   struct OnState : State
 2   {
 3     OnState() { cout << "Light turned on\n"; }
 4     void off(LightSwitch* ls) override;
 5   };
 6
 7   struct OffState : State
 8   {
 9     OffState() { cout << "Light turned off\n"; }
10     void on(LightSwitch* ls) override;
11   };
```

The implementations of OnState::off and OffState::on allow the state itself to switch itself to another state! Here's what it looks like:

```
1   void OnState::off(LightSwitch* ls)
2   {
3     cout << "Switching light off...\n";
4     ls->set_state(new OffState());
5     delete this;
6   } // same for OffState::on
```

So this is where the switching happens. This implementation contains the bizarre invocation of delete this, something you don't often see in real-world C++. delete this makes a very dangerous assumption of where the state is initially allocated. The example could be rewritten with, say, smart pointers, but using pointers and heap allocation highlights clearly that the state is being actively destroyed here. If the state had a destructor, it would trigger and you would perform additional cleanup here.

Of course, we do want the switch itself to switch states too, which looks like this:

```
1   class LightSwitch
2   {
3     ...
4     void on() { state->on(this); }
5     void off() { state->off(this); }
6   };
```

So, putting it all together, we can run the following scenario:

```
1   LightSwitch ls; // Light turned off
2   ls.on();          // Switching light on...
3                     // Light turned on
4   ls.off();         // Switching light off...
5                     // Light turned off
6   ls.off();         // Light is already off
```

262

I must admit: I don't like this approach, because it is not intuitive. Sure, the state can be informed (Observer pattern) that we're moving into it. But the idea of state switching itself to another state—which is the 'classic' implementation of the State pattern as per the GoF book—doesn't seem particularly palatable.

If we were to clumsily illustrate a transition from OffState to OnState, it needs to be illustrated as:

```
1             LightSwitch::on() -> OffState::on()
2   OffState ----------------------------------> OnState
```

On the other hand, the transition from OnState to OnState uses the base State class, the one that tells you that you are already in that state:

```
1             LightSwitch::on() -> State::on()
2   OnState ----------------------------> OnState
```

The example presented here may seem particularly artificial, so we are now going to look at another handmade set-up, one where the states and transitions are reduced to enumeration members.

Handmade State Machine

Let's try to define a state machine for a typical phone conversation. First of all, we'll describe the states of a phone:

```
1   enum class State
2   {
3     off_hook,
4     connecting,
5     connected,
6     on_hold,
7     on_hook
8   };
```

We can now also define transitions between states, also as an enum class:

```
1   enum class Trigger
2   {
3     call_dialed,
4     hung_up,
5     call_connected,
6     placed_on_hold,
7     taken_off_hold,
8     left_message,
9     stop_using_phone
10  };
```

Now, the exact *rules* of this state machine, that is, what transitions are possible, need to be stored somewhere.

```
1   map<State, vector<pair<Trigger, State>>> rules;
```

So this is a little clumsy, but essentially the key of the map is the State we're moving *from,* and the value is a set of Trigger-State pairs representing possible triggers while in this state and the state you move into when you use the trigger.

Let's initialize this data structure:

```
1   rules[State::off_hook] = {
2     {Trigger::call_dialed, State::connecting},
3     {Trigger::stop_using_phone, State::on_hook}
4   };
5
6   rules[State::connecting] = {
7     {Trigger::hung_up, State::off_hook},
8     {Trigger::call_connected, State::connected}
9   };
10  // more rules here
```

We also need a starting state, and we can also add an exit (terminal) state if we want the state machine to stop executing once that state is reached:

```
1   State currentState{ State::off_hook },
2   exitState{ State::on_hook };
```

Having made this, we don't necessarily have to build a separate component for actually running (we use the term *orchestrating*) a state machine. For example, if we wanted to build an interactive model of the telephone, we could do it thus:

```
1    while (true)
2    {
3      cout << "The phone is currently " << currentState << endl;
4    select_trigger:
5      cout << "Select a trigger:" << "\n";
6
7      int i = 0;
8      for (auto item : rules[currentState])
9      {
10       cout << i++ << ". " << item.first << "\n";
11     }
12
13     int input;
14     cin >> input;
15     if (input < 0 || (input+1) > rules[currentState].size())
16     {
17       cout << "Incorrect option. Please try again." << "\n";
18       goto select_trigger;
19     }
20
21     currentState = rules[currentState][input].second;
22     if (currentState == exitState) break;
23   }
```

First of all: yes, I do use goto, this is a good illustration of where it's appropriate. As for the algorithm itself, this is fairly obvious: we let the user select one of the available triggers on the current state (operator << has been implemented for both State and Trigger behind the scenes) and, provided the trigger is valid, we transition to it by using that rules map that we created earlier.

And if the state we've reached is the exit state, we just jump out of the loop. Here's a sample interaction with the program:

```
1    The phone is currently off the hook
2    Select a trigger:
3    0. call dialed
4    1. putting phone on hook
5    0
6    The phone is currently connecting
7    Select a trigger:
8    0. hung up
9    1. call connected
10   1
11   The phone is currently connected
12   Select a trigger:
13   0. left message
14   1. hung up
15   2. placed on hold
16   2
17   The phone is currently on hold
18   Select a trigger:
19   0. taken off hold
20   1. hung up
21   1
22   The phone is currently off the hook
```

```
23   Select a trigger:
24   0. call dialed
25   1. putting phone on hook
26   1
27   We are done using the phone
```

This hand-rolled state machine's main benefit is that it is very easy to understand: states and transitions are ordinary enumerations, the set of transitions is defined in a simple std::map, and the start and end states are simple variables.

State Machines with Boost.MSM

In the real world, state machines are more complicated. Sometimes, you want some action to occur when a state is reached. At other times, you want transitions to be *conditional*, that is, you want a transition to occur only if some condition holds.

When using Boost.MSM (Meta State Machine), a state machine library that's part of Boost, your state machine is a class that inherits from state_ machine_def via CRTP:

```
1   struct PhoneStateMachine : state_machine_def<PhoneStateMachine>
2   {
3     bool angry{ false };
```

I've added a bool indicating whether the caller is angry (e.g., at being put on hold); we'll use it a little bit later. Now, each state can also reside in the state machine, and is expected to inherit from the state class:

```
1   struct OffHook : state<> {};
2   struct Connecting : state<>
3   {
4     template <class Event, class FSM>
```

```
5      void on_entry(Event const& evt, FSM&)
6      {
7        cout << "We are connecting..." << endl;
8      }
9      // also on_exit
10   };
11   // other states omitted
```

As you can see, the state can also define behaviors that happen when you enter or exit a particular state.

You can also define behaviors to be executed on a transition (rather than when you've reached a state): these are also classes, but they don't need to inherit from anything; instead, they need to provide operator() with a particular signature:

```
1    struct PhoneBeingDestroyed
2    {
3      template <class EVT, class FSM, class SourceState, class
         TargetState>
4      void operator()(EVT const&, FSM&, SourceState&,
         TargetState&)
5      {
6        cout << "Phone breaks into a million pieces" << endl;
7      }
8    };
```

As you may have guessed, the arguments give you references to the state machine and the states you're going from and to.

Last, we have *guard conditions*: these dictate whether or not we can actually use a transition in the first place. Now, our Boolean variable angry is not in the form usable by MSM, so we need to wrap it:

```
1  struct CanDestroyPhone
2  {
3    template <class EVT, class FSM, class SourceState, class
       TargetState>
4    bool operator()(EVT const&, FSM& fsm, SourceState&,
     TargetState&)
5    {
6      return fsm.angry;
7    }
8  };
```

The preceding makes a guard condition called CanDestroyPhone, which we can later use when we define the state machine.

For defining state machine rules, Boost.MSM uses MPL (metaprogramming library). Specifically, the transition table is defined as an mpl::vector with each row containing, in turn,

- The source state

- The transition

- The target state

- An optional action to execute

- An optional guard condition

So with all of that, we can define some phone-calling rules as follows:

```
1   struct transition_table : mpl::vector <
2     Row<OffHook, CallDialed, Connecting>,
3     Row<Connecting, CallConnected, Connected>,
4     Row<Connected, PlacedOnHold, OnHold>,
5     Row<OnHold, PhoneThrownIntoWall, PhoneDestroyed,
6         PhoneBeingDestroyed, CanDestroyPhone>
7   > {};
```

In the preceding, unlike states, transitions such as CallDialed are classes that can be defined *outside* the state machine class. They don't have to inherit from any base class, and can easily be empty, but they do have to be types.

The last row of our transition_table is the most interesting: it specifies that we can only attempt to destroy phone subject to the CanDestroyPhone guard condition, and when the phone is actually being destroyed, the PhoneBeingDestroyed action should be executed.

Now, there are a couple more things we can add. First, we add the starting condition: since we're using Boost.MSM, the starting condition is a typedef, not a variable:

```
1   typedef OffHook initial_state;
```

Finally, we can define an action to occur if there are no possible transitions. It could happen! For example, after you smash the phone, you cannot use it anymore, right?

```
1   template <class FSM, class Event>
2   void no_transition(Event const& e, FSM&, int state)
3   {
4     cout << "No transition from state " << state_names[state]
5       << " on event " << typeid(e).name() << endl;
6   }
```

Boost MSM divides the state machine into the front end (that's what we just wrote) and the back end (the part that runs it). Using the back-end API, we can construct the state machine from the preceding state machine definition:

```
1    msm::back::state_machine<PhoneStateMachine> phone;
```

Now, assuming the existence of the info() function that just prints the state we're in, we can try orchestrating the following scenario:

```
1    info(); // The phone is currently off hook
2    phone.process_event(CallDialed{}); // We are connecting...
3    info(); // The phone is currently connecting
4    phone.process_event(CallConnected{});
5    info(); // The phone is currently connected
6    phone.process_event(PlacedOnHold{});
7    info(); // The phone is currently on hold
8
9    phone.process_event(PhoneThrownIntoWall{});
10   // Phone breaks into a million pieces
11
12   info(); // The phone is currently destroyed
13
14   phone.process_event(CallDialed{});
15   // No transition from state destroyed on event struct CallDialed
```

So this is how you define a more sophisticated, industry-strength state machine.

Summary

First of all, it's worth highlighting that Boost.MSM is one of two alternative state machine implemenetations in Boost, the other being Boost.Statechart. I'm pretty sure there are plenty of other state machine implementations out there.

Second, there's a lot more to state machines than that. For example, many libraries support the idea of *hierarchical* state machines: for example, a state of Sick can *contain* many different substates such as Flu or Chickenpox. If you are in state Flu, you are also assumed to be in the state Sick.

Finally, it's worth highlighting again how far modern state machines are from the State design pattern in its original form. The existence of duplicate APIs (e.g., LightSwitch::on/off vs. State::on/off) as well as the presence of self-deletion are definite code smells in my book. Don't get me wrong—the approach works, but it's unintuitive and cumbersome.

CHAPTER 22

Strategy

Suppose you decide to take an array or vector of several strings and output them as a list,

- just
- like
- this

If you think about the different output formats, you probably know that you need to take each element and output it with some additional markup. But in the case of languages such as HTML or LaTeX, the list will also need the start and end tags or markers. The processing of lists in either of these formats is at the same time similar (you need to output each item) and different (the way the items are output). Each of these can be handled with a separate Strategy.

We can formulate a strategy for rendering a list:

- Render the opening tag/element.
- For each of the list items, render that item.
- Render the closing tag/element.

Different strategies can be formulated for different output formats, and these strategies can be then fed into a general, nonchanging algorithm to generate the text.

This is yet another pattern that exists in dynamic (runtime-replaceable) and static (template-composed, fixed) incarnations. Let's take a look at both of them.

© Dmitri Nesteruk 2018

D. Nesteruk, *Design Patterns in Modern C++*, https://doi.org/10.1007/978-1-4842-3603-1_22

Dynamic Strategy

So our goal is to print a simple list of text items in the following formats:

```
1    enum class OutputFormat
2    {
3      markdown,
4      html
5    };
```

The skeleton of our strategy will be defined in the following base class:

```
1    struct ListStrategy
2    {
3      virtual void start(ostringstream& oss) {};
4      virtual void add_list_item(ostringstream& oss,
         const string& item) {};
5      virtual void end(ostringstream& oss) {};
6    };
```

Now let us jump to our text processing component. This component would have a list-specific member function called, say, append_list().

```
1    struct TextProcessor
2    {
3      void append_list(const vector<string> items)
4      {
5        list_strategy->start(oss);
6        for (auto& item : items)
7          list_strategy->add_list_item(oss, item);
8        list_strategy->end(oss);
9      }
```

```
10   private:
11     ostringstream oss;
12     unique_ptr<ListStrategy> list_strategy;
13   };
```

So we've got a buffer called oss where all the output goes, the strategy that we're using for rendering lists, and of course append_list(), which specifies the set of steps that need to be taken to actually render a list with a given strategy.

Now, pay attention here. Composition, as used in the preceding, is one of two possible options that can be taken to allow concrete implementations of a skeleton algorithm.

Instead, we could add functions such as add_list_item() as virtual members to be overridden by derived classes: that's what the Template Method pattern does.

Anyways, back to our discussion. We can now go ahead and implement different strategies for lists, such as a HtmlListStrategy:

```
1    struct HtmlListStrategy : ListStrategy
2    {
3      void start(ostringstream& oss) override
4      {
5        oss << "<ul>\n";
6      }
7      void end(ostringstream& oss) override
8      {
9        oss << "</ul>\n";
10     }
11     void add_list_item(ostringstream& oss, const
          string& item) override
```

```
12     {
13        oss << "<li>" << item << "</li>\n";
14     }
15   };
```

By implementing the overrides, we fill in the gaps that specify how to process lists. We would implement a MarkdownListStrategy in a similar fashion, but because Markdown does not need opening/closing tags, we would only override the add_list_item() function:

```
1    struct MarkdownListStrategy : ListStrategy
2    {
3      void add_list_item(ostringstream& oss,
4                         const string& item) override
5      {
6        oss << " * " << item << endl;
7      }
8    };
```

We can now start using the TextProcessor, feeding it different strategies and getting different results. For example:

```
1    TextProcessor tp;
2    tp.set_output_format(OutputFormat::markdown);
3    tp.append_list({"foo", "bar", "baz"});
4    cout << tp.str() << endl;
5
6    // Output:
7    // * foo
8    // * bar
9    // * baz
```

We can make provisions for strategies to be switchable at runtime—
this is precisely why we call this implementation a *dynamic* strategy. This
is done in the set_output_format() function, whose implementation is
trivial:

```cpp
1   void set_output_format(const OutputFormat format)
2   {
3     switch(format)
4     {
5       case OutputFormat::markdown:
6         list_strategy = make_unique<MarkdownListStrategy>();
7         break;
8       case OutputFormat::html:
9         list_strategy = make_unique<HtmlListStrategy>();
10        break;
11    }
12  }
```

Now, switching from one strategy to another is trivial, and you get to
see the results straight away:

```cpp
1   tp.clear(); // clears the buffer
2   tp.set_output_format(OutputFormat::Html);
3   tp.append_list({"foo", "bar", "baz"});
4   cout << tp.str() << endl;
5
6   // Output:
7   // <ul>
8   //   <li>foo</li>
9   //   <li>bar</li>
10  //   <li>baz</li>
11  // </ul>
```

Static Strategy

Thanks to the magic of templates, you can bake any strategy right into the type. Only minimal changes are necessary to the TextStrategy class:

```
1    template <typename LS>
2    struct TextProcessor
3    {
4      void append_list(const vector<string> items)
5      {
6        list_strategy.start(oss);
7        for (auto& item : items)
8            list_strategy.add_list_item(oss, item);
9        list_strategy.end(oss);
10     }
11     // other functions unchanged
12   private:
13     ostringstream oss;
14     LS list_strategy;
15   };
```

All that's happened in the preceding is that we added the LS template argument, made a member strategy with this type, and started using it instead of the pointer we had previously. The results of append_list() are identical:

```
1    // markdown
2    TextProcessor<MarkdownListStrategy> tpm;
3    tpm.append_list({"foo", "bar", "baz"});
4    cout << tpm.str() << endl;
5
```

```
6    // html
7    TextProcessor<HtmlListStrategy> tph;
8    tph.append_list({"foo", "bar", "baz"});
9    cout << tph.str() << endl;
```

The output from the preceding example is the same as for the dynamic strategy. Note that we've had to make two instances of TextProcessor, each with a distinct list-handling strategy.

Summary

The Strategy design pattern allows you to define a skeleton of an algorithm and then use composition to supply the missing implementation details related to a particular strategy. This approach exists in two incarnations:

- *Dynamic strategy* simply keeps a pointer/reference to the strategy being used. Want to change to a different strategy? Just change the reference. Easy!

- *Static strategy* requires that you choose the strategy at compile time and stick with it – there is no scope for changing your mind later on.

Should one use dynamic or static strategies? Well, dynamic ones allow you reconfiguration of the objects after they have been constructed. Imagine a UI setting that controls the form of the textual output: what would you rather have, a switchable TextProcessor or two variables of type TextProcessor<MarkdownStrategy> and TextProcessor<HtmlStrategy>? It's really up to you.

On a final note, you can constrain the set of strategies a type takes: instead of allowing a general ListStrategy argument, one can take an std::variant that lists the only permitted types that can be passed in.

CHAPTER 23

Template Method

The Strategy and Template Method design patterns are very similar, so much so that, just like with Factories, I would be very tempted to merge those patterns into a single Skeleton Method design pattern. I will resist the urge.

The difference between Strategy and Template Method is that Strategy uses composition (whether static or dynamic), whereas Template Method uses inheritance. But the core principle of defining the skeleton of an algorithm in one place and its implementation details in other places remains, once again observing OCP (we simply *extend* systems).

Game Simulation

Most board games are very similar: the game starts (some sort of set-up takes place), players take turns until a winner is decided, and then the winner can be announced. It doesn't matter what the game is—chess, checkers, or something else, we can define the algorithm as follows:

```
1    class Game
2    {
3      void run()
4      {
5        start();
6        while (!have_winner())
7          take_turn();
8        cout << "Player " << get_winner() << " wins.\n";
9      }
```

© Dmitri Nesteruk 2018
D. Nesteruk, *Design Patterns in Modern C++*, https://doi.org/10.1007/978-1-4842-3603-1_23

As you can see, the run() method, which runs the game, simply calls a set of other methods. Those are defined as pure virtual, and also have protected visibility so they don't get called on their own:

```
1   protected:
2     virtual void start() = 0;
3     virtual bool have_winner() = 0;
4     virtual void take_turn() = 0;
5     virtual int get_winner() = 0;
```

To be fair, some of the preceding methods, especially void-returning ones, do not necessarily have to be pure virtual. For example, if some games have no explicit start() procedure, having start() as pure virtual violates the ISP, since members that do not need it would still have to implement it. In the Strategy chapter we deliberately made a strategy with virtual no-op methods, but with Template Method, the case is not so clear cut.

Now, in addition to the preceding example, we can have certain public members that are relevant to all games: the number of players and the index of the current player:

```
1   class Game
2   {
3   public:
4     explicit Game(int number_of_players)
5       : number_of_players(number_of_players){}
6   protected:
7     int current_player{ 0 };
8     int number_of_players;
9   }; // other members omitted
```

From here on out, the Game class can be extended to implement a game of chess:

```
1    class Chess : public Game
2    {
3    public:
4      explicit Chess() : Game{ 2 } {}
5    protected:
6      void start() override {}
7      bool have_winner() override { return turns == max_turns; }
8      void take_turn() override
9      {
10        turns++;
11        current_player = (current_player + 1) % number_
           of_players;
12      }
13      int get_winner() override { return current_player;}
14    private:
15      int turns{ 0 }, max_turns{ 10 };
16    };
```

A game of chess involves two players, so that's fed into the constructor. We then proceed to override all the necessary functions, implementing some very simple simulation logic for ending the game after ten turns. Here is the output:

```
1    Starting a game of chess with 2 players
2    Turn 0 taken by player 0
3    Turn 1 taken by player 1
4    ...
5    Turn 8 taken by player 0
6    Turn 9 taken by player 1
7    Player 0 wins.
```

And that's pretty much all there is to it!

Summary

Unlike the Strategy, which uses composition and thus branches into static and dynamic variations, Template Method uses inheritance and, as a consequence, it can only be static, since there is no way to fiddle the inheritance characteristics of an object once it's been constructed.

The only design decision in a Template Method is whether you want the methods used by the Template Method to be pure virtual or actually have a body, even if that body is empty. If you foresee some methods unnecessary for *all* inheritors, go ahead and make them no-op ones.

CHAPTER 24

Visitor

Once you've got a hierarchy of types, unless you have access to the source code, it is impossible to add a function to each member of the hierarchy. This is a problem that requires some advance planning, and gives birth to the Visitor pattern.

Here's a simple example: suppose you have parsed a mathematical expression (with the use of the Interpreter pattern, of course!) composed of double values and addition operators:

```
1    (1.0 + (2.0 + 3.0))
```

This expression can be presented as a hierarchy similar to the following:

```
1    struct Expression
2    {
3      // nothing here (yet)
4    };
5
6    struct DoubleExpression : Expression
7    {
8      double value;
9      explicit DoubleExpression(const double value)
10       : value{value} {}
11   };
12
```

© Dmitri Nesteruk 2018
D. Nesteruk, *Design Patterns in Modern C++*, https://doi.org/10.1007/978-1-4842-3603-1_24

```
13    struct AdditionExpression : Expression
14    {
15      Expression *left, *right;
16
17      AdditionExpression(Expression* const left,
          Expression* const right)
18        : left{left}, right{right} {}
19
20      ~AdditionExpression()
21      {
22        delete left; delete right;
23      }
24    };
```

So, given this hierarchy of objects, suppose you want to add some behavior to the various Expression inheritors (well, we only have two for now, but this number can increase). How would you do it?

Intrusive Visitor

We'll start with the most direct approach, one that breaks the Open-Closed Principle. Essentially, we are going to jump into our already written code and modify the Expression interface (and, by association, every derived class):

```
1    struct Expression
2    {
3      virtual void print(ostringstream& oss) = 0;
4    };
```

In addition to breaking OCP, this modification hinges on the assumption that you actually have access to the hierarchy's source code —something that's not always guaranteed. But we've got to start

somewhere, right? So with this change, we need to implement print()
in DoubleExpression (that's easy, so I'll omit it here) as well as in
AdditionExpression:

```
1    struct AdditionExpression : Expression
2    {
3      Expression *left, *right;
4      ...
5      void print(ostringstream& oss) override
6      {
7        oss << "(";
8        left->print(oss);
9        oss << "+";
10       right->print(oss);
11       oss << ")";
12     }
13   };
```

Ooh, this is fun! We are polymorphically and recursively calling
print() on subexpressions. Wonderful; let's test this out:

```
1    auto e = new AdditionExpression{
2      new DoubleExpression{1},
3      new AdditionExpression{
4        new DoubleExpression{2},
5        new DoubleExpression{3}
6      }
7    };
8    ostringstream oss;
9    e->print(oss);
10   cout << oss.str() << endl; // prints (1+(2+3))
```

Well, this was easy. But now imagine you've got ten inheritors in the hierarchy (not uncommon, by the way, in real-world scenarios) and you need to add some new eval() operation. That's ten modifications that need to be done in ten different classes. But OCP isn't the real problem.

The real problem is SRP. You see, a problem such as printing is a special concern. Rather than stating that every expression should print itself, why not introduce an ExpessionPrinter that knows how to print expressions? And, later on, you can introduce an ExpressionEvaluator that knows how to perform the actual calculations, all without affecting the Expression hierarchy in any way.

Reflective Printer

Now that we've decided to make a *separate* printer component, let's get rid of print() member functions (but keep the base class, of course). There's a caveat here: you cannot leave the Expression class empty. Why? Because you only get polymorphic behavior if you actually have something virtual in it. So, for now, let's stick a virtual destructor in there; that will do!

```
1   struct Expression
2   {
3     virtual ~Expression() = default;
4   };
```

Now let's try to implement an ExpressionPrinter. My first instinct would be to write something like this:

```
1   struct ExpressionPrinter
2   {
3     void print(DoubleExpression *de, ostringstream& oss) const
4     {
5       oss << de->value;
6     }
```

```
7     void print(AdditionExpression *ae, ostringstream& oss) const
8     {
9       oss << "(";
10      print(ae->left, oss);
11      oss << "+";
12      print(ae->right, oss);
13      oss << ")";
14    }
15  };
```

Odds of the preceding code compiling: ZERO. C++ knows that, say, ae->left is an Expression, but since it doesn't check the type at runtime (unlike various dynamically typed languages), it doesn't know which overload to call. Too bad!

What can be done here? Well, only one thing – remove the overloads and check the type at runtime:

```
1   struct ExpressionPrinter
2   {
3     void print(Expression *e)
4     {
5       if (auto de = dynamic_cast<DoubleExpression*>(e))
6       {
7         oss << de->value;
8       }
9       else if (auto ae = dynamic_cast<AdditionExpression*>(e))
10      {
11        oss << "(";
12        print(ae->left, oss);
13        oss << "+";
14        print(ae->right, oss);
15        oss << ")";
```

```
16          }
17        }
18
19      string str() const { return oss.str(); }
20      private:
21        ostringstream oss;
22    };
```

The preceding is actually a usable solution:

```
1     auto e = new AdditionExpression{
2       new DoubleExpression{ 1 },
3       new AdditionExpression{
4         new DoubleExpression{ 2 },
5         new DoubleExpression{ 3 }
6       }
7     };
8     ExpressionPrinter ep;
9     ep.print(e);
10    cout << ep.str() << endl; // prints "(1+(2+3))"
```

This approach has a fairly significant downside: there are no compiler checks that you *have*, in fact, implemented printing for every single element in the hierarchy.

When a new element gets added, you can keep using ExpressionPrinter without modification, and it will just skip over any element of the new type.

But this is a viable solution. Seriously, it's quite possible to stop here and never go any further in the Visitor pattern: dynamic_cast isn't *that* expensive and I think many developers will remember to cover every single type of object in that if statement.

WTH is Dispatch?

Whenever people speak of visitors, the word *dispatch* is brought up. What it it? Well, put simply, "dispatch" is a problem of figuring out which function to call—specifically, how many pieces of information are required in order to make the call.

Here's a simple example:

```
1  struct Stuff {}
2  struct Foo : Stuff {}
3  struct Bar : Stuff {}
4
5  void func(Foo* foo) {}
6  void func(Bar* bar) {}
```

Now, if I make an ordinary Foo object, I'll have no problem calling func() with it:

```
1  Foo *foo = new Foo;
2  func(foo); // ok
```

But if I decide to cast it to a base class pointer, well, the compiler will not know which overload to call:

```
1  Stuff *stuff = new Foo;
2  func(stuff); // oops!
```

Now, let's think about this polymorphically: is there *any* way we can coerce the system to invoke the correct overload without any runtime (dynamic_cast and similar) checks? Turns out there is.

See, when you call something on a Stuff, that call *can* be polymorphic (thanks to a Vtable) and it can be dispatched right to the necessary component. Which in turn can call the necessary overload. This is called *double dispatch* because:

1. First you do a polymorphic call on the actual object.

2. Inside the polymorphic call, you call the overload. Since, inside the object, this has a precise type (e.g., a Foo* or Bar*), the right overload is triggered.

Here's what I mean:

```
1   struct Stuff {
2     virtual void call() = 0;
3   }
4   struct Foo : Stuff {
5     void call() override { func(this); }
6   }
7   struct Bar : Stuff {
8     void call() override { func(this); }
9   }
10
11  void func(Foo* foo) {}
12  void func(Bar* bar) {}
```

Can you see what's happening here? We cannot just stick one generic call() implemenetation into Stuff: the distinct implementations *must* bein their respective classes so that the this pointer is suitably typed.

This implentation lets you write the following:

```
1   Stuff *stuff = new Foo;
2   stuff->call(); // effectively calls func(stuff);
```

Classic Visitor

The "classic" implementation of the Visitor design pattern uses double dispatch. There are conventions as to what the visitor member functions are called:

- Member functions of the visitor are typically called `visit()`.

- Member functions implemented throughout the hierarchy are typically called `accept()`.

We can now throw away that virtual destructor from our `Expression` base class because we've actually got something to put in there: the `accept()` function:

```
1    struct Expression
2    {
3      virtual void accept(ExpressionVisitor *visitor) = 0;
4    };
```

As you can see, the preceding refers to an (abstract) class named `ExpressionVisitor` that can serve as a base class for various visitors such as `ExpressionPrinter`, `ExpressionEvaluator`, and similar. I've chosen to take a pointer here, but you can use a reference instead.

Now, every single inheritor of `Expression` is now *required* to implement `accept()` in an identical way, namely:

```
1    void accept(ExpressionVisitor* visitor) override
2    {
3      visitor->visit(this);
4    }
```

On the other side, we can define the ExpressionVisitor as follows:

```
1    struct ExpressionVisitor
2    {
3      virtual void visit(DoubleExpression* de) = 0;
4      virtual void visit(AdditionExpression* ae) = 0;
5    };
```

Notice that we *absolutely must* define overloads for all objects; otherwise, we would get a compilation error when implementing the corresponding accept(). We can now inherit from this class to define our ExpressionPrinter:

```
1    struct ExpressionPrinter : ExpressionVisitor
2    {
3      ostringstream oss;
4      string str() const { return oss.str(); }
5      void visit(DoubleExpression* de) override;
6      void visit(AdditionExpression* ae) override;
7    };
```

The implementation of the visit() functions should be fairly obvious, since we've seen it more than once already, but I'll show it once again:

```
1    void ExpressionPrinter::visit(AdditionExpression* ae)
2    {
3      oss << "(";
4      ae->left->accept(this);
5      oss << "+";
6      ae->right->accept(this);
7      oss << ")";
8    }
```

Notice how the calls now happen *on* the subexpressions themselves, leveraging double dispatch once again. As for the usage of the new double dispatch Visitor, here it is:

```
1    void main()
2    {
3      auto e = new AdditionExpression{
4        // as before
5      };
6      ostringstream oss;
7      ExpressionPrinter ep;
8      ep.visit(e);
9      cout << ep.str() << endl; // (1+(2+3))
10   }
```

Implementing an Additional Visitor

So, what is the advantage of this approach? The advantage is you have to implement the accept() member through the hierarchy *just once*. You'll never have to touch a member of the hierarchy again. For example: suppose you now want to have a way of evaluating the result of the expression? This is easy:

```
1    struct ExpressionEvaluator : ExpressionVisitor
2    {
3      double result;
4      void visit(DoubleExpression* de) override;
5      void visit(AdditionExpression* ae) override;
6    };
```

but one needs to keep in mind that visit() is currently declared as a void method, so the implementation might look a little bit weird:

```
1   void ExpressionEvaluator::visit(DoubleExpression* de)
2   {
3     result = de->value;
4   }
5
6   void ExpressionEvaluator::visit(AdditionExpression* ae)
7   {
8     ae->left->accept(this);
9     auto temp = result;
10    ae->right->accept(this);
11    result += temp;
12  }
```

The preceding is a by product of an inability to return from accept() and is a little bit tricky. Essentially, we evaluate the left part and cache the value. Then we evaluate the right part (so result is set), then increase it by the value we cached, thereby producing the sum. Not exactly intuitive code!

Still, it works just fine:

```
1   auto e = new AdditionExpression{ /* as before */ };
2   ExpressionPrinter printer;
3   ExpressionEvaluator evaluator;
4   printer.visit(e);
5   evaluator.visit(e);
6   cout << printer.str() << " = " << evaluator.result << endl;
7   // prints "(1+(2+3)) = 6"
```

And, in the same vein, you can add lots of other different visitors, honoring OCP and having fun in the process.

Acyclic Visitor

Now is a good time to mention that there are actually two strains, if you will, of the Visitor design pattern. They are

- **Cyclic Visitor**, which is based on function overloading. Due to the cyclic dependency between the hierarchy (which must be aware of the visitor's type) and the visitor (which must be aware of *every* class in the hierarchy), the use of the approach is limited to stable hierarchies that are infrequently updated.

- **Acyclic Visitor**, which is based on RTTI. The advantage here is the absence of limitations on visited hierarchies but, as you may have guessed, there are performance implications.

The first step in the implementation of the Acyclic Visitor is the actual visitor interface. Instead of defining a visit() overload for every single type in the hierarchy, we make things as generic as possible:

```
1    template <typename Visitable>
2    struct Visitor
3    {
4      virtual void visit(Visitable& obj) = 0;
5    };
```

We need each element in our domain model to be able to accept such a visitor but, since every specialization is unique, what we do is introduce a *marker interface*—an empty class nothing but a virtual destructor:

```
1    struct VisitorBase // marker interface
2    {
3      virtual ~VisitorBase() = default;
4    };
```

297

The preceding class has no behavior, but we *will* use it as an argument to an accept() method in whichever object we want to actually visit. Now, what we can do is redefine our Expression class from before as follows:

```
1   struct Expression
2   {
3     virtual ~Expression() = default;
4
5     virtual void accept(VisitorBase& obj)
6     {
7       using EV = Visitor<Expression>;
8       if (auto ev = dynamic_cast<EV*>(&obj))
9         ev->visit(*this);
10    }
11  };
```

So here's how the new accept() method works: we take a VisitorBase but then try to cast it to a Visitor<T>, where T is the type we're currently in. If the cast succeeds, the visitor in question knows how to visit our type, and so we call its visit() method. If it fails, it's a no-op. It is *critical* to understand why obj itself does not have a visit() that we could call on it. If it did, it would require an overload for every single type that would be interested in calling it, which is precisely what introduces a cyclic dependency.

After implementing accept() in other parts of our model, we can put everything together by once again defining an ExpressionPrinter, but this time round, it would look as follows:

```
1   struct ExpressionPrinter : VisitorBase,
2                              Visitor<DoubleExpression>,
3                              Visitor<AdditionExpression>
4   {
5     void visit(DoubleExpression &obj) override;
6     void visit(AdditionExpression &obj) override;
7
```

```
8      string str() const { return oss.str(); }
9   private:
10     ostringstream oss;
11   };
```

As you can see, we implement the VisitorBase marker interface as well as a Visitor<T> for every T that we like to visit. If we omit a particular type T (for example, suppose I comment out Visitor<DoubleExpression>), the program will still compile, and the corresponding accept() call, if it comes, will simply execute as a no-op.

In the preceding, the implementations of the visit() methods are virtually identical to what we had in the Classic visitor implementation, and so are the results.

Variants and `std::visit`

While not directly related to the classic Visitor pattern, it's worth mentioning std::visit, if only because its name suggests something to do with the Visitor pattern. Essentially, std::visit is a way of accessing the correct part of a variant type.

Here's an example: suppose you have an address, and part of that address is a house field. Now, a house can be just a number (as in "123 London Road") or it can have a name such as "Montefiore Castle." So you can define the variant as follows:

```
1   variant<string, int> house;
2   // house = "Montefiore Castle";
3   house = 221;
```

Either of the two assignments are valid. Now, suppose you decide to print the house name or number. To do this, you can first define a type that has function call overloads for the different types of members inside the variant:

```
1    struct AddressPrinter
2    {
3      void operator()(const string& house_name) const {
4        cout << "A house called " << house_name << "\n";
5      }
6
7      void operator()(const int house_number) const {
8        cout << "House number " << house_number << "\n";
9      }
10   };
```

Now, this type can be used in conjunction with std::visit(), a library function that applies this visitor to the variant type:

```
1    AddressPrinter ap;
2    std::visit(ap, house); // House number 221
```

It's also possible to define the set of visitor functions in place, thanks to some Modern C++ magic. What we need to do is construct a lambda with type of auto&, get the underlying type, compare it using if constexpr, and process accordingly:

```
1    std::visit([](auto& arg) {
2      using T = decay_t<decltype(arg)>;
3
4      if constexpr (is_same_v<T, string>)
5      {
6        cout << "A house called " << arg.c_str() << "\n";
7      }
```

```
 8      else
 9      {
10         cout << "House number " << arg << "\n";
11      }
12   }, house);
```

Summary

The Visitor design pattern allows us to add some behavior to every element in a hierarchy of objects. The approaches we have seen include

- *Intrusive*: adding a virtual method to every single object in the hierarchy. Possible (assuming you have access to source code) but breaks OCP.

- *Reflective*: adding a separate visitor that requires no changes to the objects; uses dynamic_cast whenever runtime dispatch is needed.

- *Classic*(double dispatch): the entire hierarchy *does* get modified, but just once and in a very generic way. Each element of the hierarchy learns to accept() a visitor. We then subclass the visitor to enhance the hierarchy's functionality in all sorts of directions.

The Visitor appears quite often in tandem with the Interpreter pattern: having interpreted some textual input and transformed it into object-oriented structures, we need to, for example, render the abstract syntax tree in a particular way. Visitor helps propagate an ostringstream (or similar object) throughout the entire hierarchy and collate the data together.

PART IV

Appendix A: Functional Design Patterns

While C++ is primarily an object-oriented programming language, the support of functional objects (e.g., `std::function`) together with lambda functions gives it limited support for monads, which are design patterns of the functional programming world. It has to be said, though, that monads are much more usable in functional programing languages thanks to better treatment of functional objects as well as useful auxiliary constructs (e.g., algebraic data types, pattern matching, etc.).

It is not my intention to show a catalogue of monads in this book, but I do want to show at least one example of a monad that can be used by C++ developers.

CHAPTER 25

Maybe Monad

In C++, like in many other languages, we have different ways of expressing the presence or absence of a value. In C++ specifically, we can use any of the following:

- Using `nullptr` to encode absence.

- Using a smart pointer (e.g., `shared_ptr`) which, again, can be tested for presence or absence.

- `std::optional<T>` is a library solution; it can either store a value of type T or `std::nullopt` if the value is missing.

Suppose we decide to go with the `nullptr` approach. In this case, let's imagine that our domain model defines a `Person` who may or may not have an `Address`, which, in turn, can have an optional house_name[1]:

```
1   struct Address {
2       string* house_name = nullptr;
3   };
4
5   struct Person {
6       Address* address = nullptr;
7   };
```

---

[1]House names are a real thing (at least in the UK): when you buy a castle, its address is not "123 London Road," it's simply "Montefiore Castle" and that is its address. As you can guess, not all houses have names, which explains why this field is optional.

D. Nesteruk, *Design Patterns in Modern C++*, https://doi.org/10.1007/978-1-4842-3603-1_25

What we are interested in is writing a function that, given a person, *safely* prints the house name of that person, if it exists of course. In "conventional" C++ we would implement it like so:

```
1   void print_house_name(Person* p)
2   {
3     if (p != nullptr &&
4        p->address != nullptr &&
5        p->address->house_name != nullptr) // ugh!
6       cout << *p->address->house_name << endl;
7   }
```

The preceding code represents the process of *drilling down* into an object's structure, being careful not to access nullptr values. It is this process of drilling down that can, instead, be represented in a functional way by the use of a *Maybe Monad*.

To construct the monad, we are going to define a new type Maybe<T>. This type is going to be used as a temporary object that participates in the drilling-down process:

```
1   template <typename T> struct Maybe {
2     T* context;
3     Maybe(T *context) : context(context) { }
4   };
```

So far, Maybe looks like a pointer container, nothing exciting. It's also not very usable because, given a Person* p, we cannot make a Maybe(p) due to our inability to deduce class template parameters from arguments passed in the constructor. In this case, we also make a helper global function because a function *can*, in fact, deduce the template argument:

```
1   template <typename T> Maybe<T> maybe(T* context)
2   {
3     return Maybe<T>(context);
4   }
```

Now, what we want to do is to give Maybe a member function that

- Drills deeper into the object if context != nullptr; or

- Does nothing if the context is, in fact, nullptr

The process of "drilling down" is encapsulated into a template parameter Func as follows:

```
1   template <typename Func>
2   auto With(Func evaluator)
3   {
4     return context != nullptr ? maybe(evaluator(context)) :
      nullptr;
5   }
```

The preceding is an example of a *higher-order function*, that is, a function that takes a function.[2] This function we've created takes another function called evaluator which, given that the current context is non-null, can be called on a context and return a pointer that can be wrapped in another Maybe. This trick allows the chaining of With() calls.

Now, in a similar fashion, we can make yet another member function, this time simply invoking the given function on the context without changing the context itself:

```
1   template <typename TFunc>
2   auto Do(TFunc action)
3   {
4     if (context != nullptr) action(context);
5     return *this;
6   }
```

---

[2]Strictly speaking, a higher-order function is a function that either *takes* a funcrion as one or more parameters or *returns* a function (or both).

And we're done! What we can now do is redefine our print_house_name() function to the following:

```
1    void print_house_name(Person* p)
2    {
3      auto z = maybe(p)
4          .With([](auto x) { return x->address; })
5          .With([](auto x) { return x->house_name; })
6          .Do([](auto x) { cout << *x << endl; });
7    }
```

There are a few things to note here. First of all, we managed to create a *fluent interface*, that is, a set-up where function calls can be chained one after another. This kind of makes sense, since each operator (With, Do, etc.) returns either *this or a new Maybe<T>. Also worth noting is how the drill-down process is encapsulated at each turn by a lambda function.

As you can probably guess, the preceding approach does have performance costs, though those costs are difficult to predict and depend on how well the compiler is able to optimize code. It's also far from perfect, as I would be very happy to omit the [](auto x) part in favor of some shorthand notation. Ideally, something like maybe(p).With{it->address} would be nice.[3]

---

[3]This approach is supported, for example, by the Kotlin and Swift programming languages. Both of these languages allow the programmer to avoid the extra lambda-function ceremony if it is not necessary. This includes the omission of parameters, capture list and return value, as well as the use of curly braces, as opposed to round brackets, which lets you simply open a de facto scope and place all the statements to be executed by the lambda.

Index

A

Abstract factory, 56–59
Abstract syntax tree (AST), 198–199
Adapter
    LineToPointAdapter, 92, 94
    rectangles, 91, 93
    scenario, 89–91
    temporaries
        Boost's hash functions, 96
        DrawPoints(), 94
        hash functions and
          caching, 97
        ReSharper's Generate | Hash
          function, 95
add_child(), 36
Array-backed properties, 108–111

B

BetterFormattedText, 145
Boost.Serialization, 69
Boost's hash functions, 96
Bridge
    C++ compilers, 99
    circle, 103–104
    Pimpl idiom, 102
    RasterRenderer, 105
    Renderer base class, 102
    Shape class, 103

Builder pattern
    add_child() method, 35, 36
    static build() function, 38
    communicating intent, 37–38
    complicated objects, 33
    composite (*see* Composite
        builder)
    groovy-style, 39–41
    HtmlElement class, 34, 38

C

Chain of responsibility (CoR)
    broker chain, 166–167, 169
    characteristic values, 161
    CreatureModifier, 162
    pointer chain, 162–165
CLion, 68, 74
Code generation tools, 74
Command design pattern
    composite command,
        180–183
    CQS, 183–184, 186
    deposit() and withdraw()
        functions, 173–174
    implementation, 175–176
    undo operations, 176–178, 180
Command Query Separation
    (CQS), 183–187

V, W, X, Y, Z

Get the eBook for only $5!

Why limit yourself?

With most of our titles available in both PDF and ePUB format, you can access your content wherever and however you wish—on your PC, phone, tablet, or reader.

Since you've purchased this print book, we are happy to offer you the eBook for just $5.

To learn more, go to http://www.apress.com/companion or contact support@apress.com.

Apress®